"If you've ever felt like your creative energy and your motherhood were at odds, *Create Anyway* will be a balm to your soul. Ashlee's personal experiences and thoughtful insight, paired with creative exercises and journaling prompts, are sure to remind your heart that creating in the margins is worth the effort it takes!"

—Ruth Chou Simons, mom to six boys, *Wall Street Journal* bestselling author, and founder of gracelaced.com

"*Create Anyway* is an anthem, an invitation, a spark that will light a fire in your heart. As a mom to three littles with a busy schedule and a list of excuses as to why this season isn't suited for making art, I needed this permission slip to pick up my pen and do exactly what Ashlee encourages mothers to do—create anyway."

—Gretchen Saffles, founder of Well-Watered Women and bestselling author of *The Well-Watered Woman*

"This book is a love letter. A love letter that will be bookmarked, dog-eared, highlighted, and scribbled in for years to come—throughout all the messy and gritty states of motherhood. As a mom of an emerging two-year-old, I didn't realize (but God knew) how much I needed to read these words. Every page, story, and anecdote spoke to me. If you're looking for a manual to help you reclaim the sacred slowness of motherhood and creativity, pick this one up today. You will find yourself breathing easier after just the first chapter."

—Hannah Brencher, author of *Fighting Forward* and *Come Matter Here*

"As a long-time friend of Ashlee Gadd, I can tell you she lives out the words on these pages. The stories and wisdom in *Create Anyway* will inspire you to prioritize and delight in making art, not in spite of motherhood, but because of it. She's the cheerleader we all need."

—Laura Wifler, author, podcaster, and cofounder of Risen Motherhood

"I cried tears of release throughout this book. It's dreamy and gorgeous and raw, and I feel as if I can finally exhale after two long, hard years.

Thank you, Ashlee, for reminding me that I have permission to create just as God intended."

—Leslie Means, creator of Her View From Home

"I dare you not to be refreshed after reading this. Part pep talk, part permission slip, this beautiful book honors both the mothering journey *and* our God-given desires to create. Ashlee's honest reflections will leave you encouraged and affirmed. I'll be placing *Create Anyway* in the hands of women for years to come."

—Kayla Craig, author of *To Light Their Way* and creator of Liturgies for Parents

"With wit, wisdom, and a wealth of grace, Ashlee Gadd woos us to believe that motherhood and creativity do not detract from each other. Indeed, they deepen each other. *Create Anyway* is a compassionate call to be enchanted by the ordinary and see the beauty right where you belong. Ashlee's stories are a sacred invitation, welcoming all of us—in spite of all that feels hard and hopeless—to create anyway."

—Rachel Marie Kang, founder of The Fallow House and author of *Let There Be Art*

"Imagine one giant exhale, taking a refreshing shower, and drinking a cold glass of water. This is what reading *Create Anyway* feels like. If you've ever questioned your value or worth in the long season of mothering little ones, I highly recommend this book! It feels like letting go and coming home at the same time."

—Anjuli Paschall, author of *Stay* and *Awake*

"*Create Anyway* is a glimpse into where the good stuff is made—under the piles of laundry, runny noses, and lists that never seem to end. Sharing her own relatable stories, Ashlee drops breadcrumbs of hope, confirming that we are not alone in the messy margins and perhaps instead of waiting for 'perfect' we have permission to lean in and make something beautiful right there."

—Jena Holliday, artist, author, and founder of Spoonful of Faith

CREATE ANYWAY

CREATE ANYWAY

The Joy of Pursuing Creativity in the
Margins of Motherhood

ASHLEE GADD

BETHANYHOUSE
a division of Baker Publishing Group
Minneapolis, Minnesota

Published by Bethany House Publishers
Minneapolis, Minnesota
www.bethanyhouse.com

Bethany House Publishers is a division of
Baker Publishing Group, Grand Rapids, Michigan

Printed in China

Library of Congress Cataloging-in-Publication Data
Names: Gadd, Ashlee, author.
Title: Create anyway : the joy of pursuing creativity in the margins of
    motherhood / Ashlee Gadd.
Description: Minneapolis, Minnesota : Bethany House Publishers, a division of
    Baker Publishing Group, 2023.
Identifiers: LCCN 2022024908 | ISBN 9780764240041 (cloth) | ISBN
    9781493440788 (ebook)
Subjects: LCSH: Creation (Literary, artistic, etc.)—Religious aspects—
    Christianity. | Motherhood—Religious aspects—Christianity.
Classification: LCC BT709.5 .G33 2023 | DDC 248.8/431—dc23/eng/20220722
LC record available at https://lccn.loc.gov/2022024908

Unless otherwise indicated, Scripture quotations are from The Holy Bible, English Standard Version® (ESV®), copyright © 2001 by Crossway, a publishing ministry of Good News Publishers. Used by permission. All rights reserved. ESV Text Edition: 2016

Scripture quotations labeled NIV are from THE HOLY BIBLE, NEW INTERNATIONAL VERSION®, NIV® Copyright © 1973, 1978, 1984, 2011 by Biblica, Inc.® Used by permission. All rights reserved worldwide.

Cover design by Kathleen Lynch/Black Kat Design

Unless otherwise noted, the photos in this book were taken by Ashlee Gadd. The artist photos are from the artists themselves, except for Rachel Kang's, which was taken by Shin Sung Kang. The author photo on p. 250 was taken by Danielle Kelley, D. Lillian Photography.

Published in association with Illuminate Literary Agency, www.illuminateliterary .com.

Baker Publishing Group publications use paper produced from sustainable forestry practices and post-consumer waste whenever possible.

23 24 25 26 27 28 29   7 6 5 4 3 2 1

for Everett, Carson, and Presley—
I loved writing this book, but I love being your mom more.

and for Katie—
who's had every reason to give up,
but keeps creating anyway.

Mothers shape love and macaroni and

sleeplessness and soap into young men

and women over the course of many years;

is there a greater art, or a more powerful

patient creativity, than *that*?

—Brian Doyle

CONTENTS

A NOTE ABOUT THE PHOTOS IN THIS BOOK

The year I wrote this book, I learned how to shoot film. I started at the beginning with Google and YouTube and a used camera I bought off Ebay. I kid you not: it took me thirty minutes to figure out how to load film in the camera.

Unlike digital photography—which is quick and efficient—film is both painfully slow and wildly obscure. You cannot course correct if your settings are wrong, because you don't actually *know* your settings are wrong until you get the pictures back.

At the same time, film offers wonder and mystery, enchantment and grit. Film beckons me to slow down, wait for the light, wait for the moment. Wait, wait, wait. Film is teaching me the beauty of delayed gratification, a long-lost virtue in our instant-everything world.

Every photo I took for this book is one I shot on film. These images represent a humble beginning, a willingness to fail, and plenty of mistakes made. Even now I am tempted to be critical, to assure you I could have taken superior photos with a digital camera. But I suppose that's the whole point. Film, like all of creativity, requires surrender, releasing our work into the world knowing it is not perfect, and perhaps even, the extra grain is what makes it special.

These images represent my own curiosity and the courage to try something new. Which, come to think of it, is exactly what this book is about.

INTRODUCTION

My daughter Presley is playing in the bathtub, content with a plastic dinosaur and a Hot Wheels car, which, apparently, suffice as "bath toys" by third child standards.

I am sitting on a small plastic stool next to her, hunched over a stack of multicolored index cards, jotting down every parallel between motherhood and creativity I can think of: fear, comparison, imposter syndrome, sacrifice.

Presley flashes me a mischievous smile, holding a small purple Stegosaurus above her head. She babbles something incoherent before dropping it in the water—*plunk!*—flinging droplets on my cards. In case this isn't obvious, I did not write this book in a cabin in the woods.

As a little girl, that's how I thought books were written—in complete and utter solitude, at a charming wooden desk in a rustic cabin, next to a fireplace while snow fell silently outside the window. Even as a teenager, if you had asked me to describe a working author, I would have conjured up a romantic scene, something picturesque, poetic, the stuff you see in movies.

In reality, I started writing this book on the bathroom floor. No desk, no cabin, no fireplace, no silence. Just me, sitting next to the tub, while my daughter splashed water on my freshly inked ideas.

I wrote this book in tiny chunks throughout my days. Sometimes inspiration struck while I stood at the kitchen counter making peanut butter and jelly sandwiches. Sentences often swirled in my head while I vacuumed Cheerios out of the carpet. I scribbled words in a tattered notebook in between breastfeeding, changing diapers, and managing distance learning for two kids in the middle of a global pandemic. Every morning, before touching my inbox or scrambling eggs, I wrote in the dark next to a burning candle before my children woke up.

And, I'll be honest, there were times I desperately wished for a cabin in the woods (for writing, yes, but also for sleeping and showering and watching Netflix and eating without a grabby toddler asking for "Mo? Mo?" bites of my food).

Then again, I don't know how I would possibly write a book about pursuing creativity in the margins, without, you know, *actually writing it in the margins.*

I used to believe motherhood and creativity were opposing forces—that my mothering was in the way of my creative work, and my creative work was in the way of my mothering.

But over the past nine years, as I've brought three babies into the world while simultaneously pursuing a number of creative endeavors, I've realized motherhood *inspires* creativity, and likewise, creativity inspires motherhood. The more I lean into both of these roles, the more I see how much they sustain each other. Both motherhood and

Both motherhood and creativity have taught me to be brave, to relentlessly seek beauty and joy among the mundane, to notice the remarkable grace flooding my unremarkable life.

creativity have taught me to be brave, to relentlessly seek beauty and joy among the mundane, to notice the remarkable grace flooding my unremarkable life.

This balancing act is not always easy or effortless. On the contrary, creating while mothering requires intention, patience, discipline, and faith. I've been tempted to give up more than once, but something inside me—a force that could only be from God Himself—propels me to keep going. To write a sentence down before I crawl into bed. To grab my camera anytime light flickers on the floor. To color and bake and arrange flowers in a jar, to do whatever it takes to keep making beautiful things in a broken world.

People often say you should write the book you want to read, and that's what I've attempted to do here. This is the book I wanted to read nine years ago, when I first became a mother and wondered if I could still pursue my creative dreams. This is the book I wanted to read seven years ago, when a little idea I had in the shower exploded in the most unexpected way. This is the book I wanted to read two weeks ago, when I wondered, for the billionth time, if any of my art mattered.

You'll notice I use the terms *creativity, creative work,* and *making art* somewhat interchangeably throughout this book. I feel it is important to disclose that at this point in my life, creativity is part of my actual job and something I get paid to do. Having said that, even now, I engage in plenty of creative acts I do not get paid for: taking pictures of my children, tending to plants in the yard, decorating my home, writing for my personal blog, hosting parties, putting together an outfit, styling bookshelves, trying new recipes, making gifts, etc. When I speak of creativity in this book, I am speaking broadly and generally of *any* creative act, whether paid or unpaid, seen or unseen, the kind of creativity that receives public accolades or the kind that simply brings a smile to your face in the privacy of your home. One is not superior to the other. If anything, I hope to convince you in the following pages that creativity is essential to our human flourishing, and therefore worth pursuing whether or not you receive payment or applause as a result.

A few months ago, standing in the Target parking lot at the end of a terrible day, I looked up and saw a bright electric-orange cloud in the sky, perfectly positioned above my car.

I cannot explain the science behind why the cloud appeared so unbelievably orange. It probably had something to do with the location of the sun, combined with the smoky haze rising from wildfires raging nearby. What I *can* tell you is this: I couldn't take my eyes off that cloud. It felt as if God had planted it there just for me, beckoning my attention. As if to say, *Hey daughter, look up! I'm with you right now. I see you right now.*

I grabbed my phone from my purse, pointing it up in the air to take a picture. And right there, standing in the Target parking lot, staring at a magnificent orange cloud in the sky, I felt wholly, completely, undeniably in the presence of God.

I couldn't help but think, This *is what it means to be an artist.*

If I could summarize this entire book in a single visual, it would be the headline from that scene: "Weary and defeated mother steps away from shopping cart in Target parking lot to document a spectacular orange cloud in the sky."

This book is about looking for hope when we feel hopeless, searching for light when the day seems dark. This book is about paying attention to beauty and mercy and grace, and then sharing those gifts with the world through our words, our paintings, our music, our photographs.

I come to you not as an expert pushing formulas or prescriptions, but simply as a friend imperfectly living out the message of this book as she writes it. While writing this book, God provided ample (and I mean *ample*!) opportunities for me to practice what I preach. I wrote the chapter on imposter syndrome while feeling like I had somehow conned my way into a book contract. I wrote the chapter on making space for creativity during a global pandemic, when I often wrote in my car, parked in the driveway, the only place I could be alone. Halfway through writing the chapter on rest, I suffered a miscarriage, forcing me to set down the entire manuscript for almost two weeks as I began to recover physically, mentally, and emotionally.

I still have days when, probably just like you, I am tempted to give up creativity altogether. Days when I desperately want to write, but my daughter refuses to nap. Or days when I finally sit down in front of a blank page, but, two hours later, have nothing to show for myself. Other days, I can become paralyzed with comparison, watching everyone around me create bigger, better, more dazzling things than I will ever make.

But I also know what exists on the other side of those stumbling blocks. Obedience. Wholeness. Fulfillment and delight. I know what it's like to co-create with God, to dream and wonder, to see glorious potential in a pile of scraps. As Makoto Fujimura says, the act of making helps us know the Creator.[1]

Therefore, I press on.

Not because I'm self-assured or fearless, but because creativity is one way I draw closer to my Maker, the same One who gave me these children and these talents. The same One who calls us to be good stewards of everything He places in our hands.

Erwin Raphael McManus writes in *The Artisan Soul*, "To leave our gifts and talents unmastered and undeveloped is to leave unwrapped precious treasures entrusted to us."[2]

My hope and prayer for you as you read this book, and long after you leave its pages, is that you would leave no treasure unwrapped. And that you would, as my pal Steph Smith says, feel me rooting for your becoming on every page.[3]

So please, dear friend—grab your journal, your instrument, your measuring cups, your camera, whatever you need right here, right now, for *your* creative gifts to shine.

This is your permission slip to write on index cards next to the tub. To bake a strawberry cake while the baby naps. To crochet a scarf on the sidelines of soccer practice.

I know your hands are full. I know you have traces of applesauce smeared on your shirt. I know there are one thousand excuses for why you don't have time to pursue creativity in this season. But I promise you: the journey is worthwhile. I can't wait to show you why.

Here's to creating in the margins.

Here's to creating anyway.

1

A PERMISSION SLIP

It's the hour right before dinner, the same hour hungry bellies and restlessness often collide in our house. Today, though, in the thick of our mild California winter, we're all grateful for the sunlight pouring through the windows, lighting up our dining room table like a stage.

Nine-year-old Everett hovers at the left corner, lining up various LEGO buildings he carefully transported inside the house from a table in the garage. Carson, seven, sits adjacent, leaning his chair back against the window, creating a comic book titled *Dogman and the Scary Kittens* with a single yellow pencil. Next to Carson, two-year-old Presley sits on her knees, dutifully peeling the wrappers off every crayon in a small plastic container in front of her. Occasionally she breaks a crayon in half and scribbles a dramatic line across a sheet of printer paper. I am tempted to reprimand her, but the act of stripping and breaking the crayons seems to be an essential part of her artistic process.

And then there's me, smooshed at the end of the table within a tiny sliver of space. My laptop is open to iMovie, a program I taught myself

how to use almost a decade ago when I wanted to make a compilation video for Everett's first birthday. I always thought my husband and I would cherish these videos the most, but the kids seem to love them even more than we do. Today I'm working on Presley's birthday video, stitching together dozens of clips to play alongside the song I've chosen—"Mama's Sunshine, Daddy's Rain" by Drew Holcomb and the Neighbors.

My eyes scan the table, and I can't help but notice the mess surrounding me: LEGOS, books, papers, colored pencils, and naked crayons. Presley is now making a small mountain out of her shredded crayon wrappers. The way the afternoon sunlight hits the top of her pile, it almost looks like a volcano.

A few weeks ago, I bought a gorgeous cream-colored linen table runner at a local home store sample sale. It was one of those purchases you think might change your life, or at least the entire aesthetic of your dining room. For exactly one week, our table looked like something you'd see on Pinterest, complete with a curated centerpiece of candles and fresh eucalyptus.

I forgot people actually live here.

Day after day, the runner and its contents got swept aside in favor of space for creative projects: theirs and mine. I remember feeling a flash of irritation the day I finally scrapped my carefully styled decor, but today, looking around this worn and cluttered table, I am content with the work happening here. Concentration. Imagination. Curiosity. The scene doesn't last long. Within minutes, tummies are growling for dinner, and the novelty of destroying crayons has worn off. But I take a split second to breathe this moment in, to notice the energy in the room as all of us create at the same table, at the same time, enveloped in warm, golden light.

For once, I don't feel the need to abandon this setup, to go start dinner or sort mail or fold laundry while my kids are temporarily occupied. I don't feel the need to assist them either, to hover or micromanage their activities. Rather, I simply feel at ease, as if this is *exactly* what I should be doing in this moment: working on my own creative project while my children work on theirs. I do not feel guilty for being on my laptop in front of my kids, nor do I feel a mounting pressure to be doing something more productive with my time.

Instead, I know for a fact this moment of creating—in front of my kids, alongside my kids—is important and worthwhile and good.

It only took me a decade to believe this.

IN THOSE FIRST FEW WEEKS AT HOME with a milk-drunk newborn in my arms, I Googled every little thing, hopping in and out of online parenting forums, desperate for an instruction manual. *Is it normal for a baby to poop six times in one day? Does breastfeeding ever get easier?* Underneath my nitty-gritty questions loomed the ultimate insecurity every first-time mom battles: *Am I doing this whole motherhood thing right?*

Just a few months prior, I had quit my pencil-skirt-and-high-heels-wearing marketing job to pursue writing and photography. Within the span of a single year, I traded cubicle life for freelance gigs and my childless freedom for motherhood. In my head, I envisioned myself slipping into these new professional and personal roles gracefully, the way a ballerina glides across a stage. In actuality, the transition looked more like an overly confident kid falling off a skateboard.

I struggled with loneliness. At the time, my husband, Brett, commuted an hour to and from work, leaving me home alone with our son, Everett, from roughly seven in the morning to six in the evening. Our days were quiet, monotonous, and unseen. Sometimes we only left the house for a brief walk around the neighborhood.

I think I had been a parent for roughly thirty-six hours when it dawned on me: motherhood doesn't come with permission slips.

Around that time, I discovered podcasts and began popping head-phones in my ears on our daily walks, eager to listen to my "friends on the Internet" who didn't know me at all. I loved being home with my son, a privilege I did not take for granted, but most days, I felt utterly invisible. I missed having coworkers. I also missed the proverbial gold stars and the swell of pride I'd feel after being told "Great job."

Perhaps even more than that, though, I missed the comfort of hav-ing a supervisor sign off on my decisions. I craved a nod of approval to accompany the sudden multitude of parenting choices I made each day. A safety net to fall into from time to time.

Having a boss seems like a weird thing to miss, but I often did. And not just because I wanted someone to cover for me on sick days or pat me on the back after I handled an explosive diaper change. Sometimes I simply wished for someone to grant me permission, for someone to whisper, "It's okay to _____."

It's okay to ask for help.

It's okay to eat cereal for dinner.

It's okay to write while the baby naps, even though the house is a disaster.

I think I had been a parent for roughly thirty-six hours when it dawned on me: motherhood doesn't come with permission slips.

PERMISSION SLIPS FOR MOTHERS

Permission to leave dishes in the sink

Permission to ask for help

Permission to cry in the shower

Permission to say no

Permission to say yes

Permission to rest

Permission to play

Permission to eat cereal for dinner

Permission to outsource

Permission to feel your feelings

Permission to step away from social media

Permission to be a beginner

Permission to not love every second of motherhood

Permission to change your mind

Permission to ask for time alone

Permission to create with no end goal in mind

DAYS AFTER EVERETT TURNED THREE, he gave up his nap cold turkey. *Poof!* Just like that. As a first-time mom, I didn't really know when children stopped napping, but after a few rough weeks for both of us, I realized *I* wasn't ready for naptime to end. So, I did what any other former marketing professional would do: *I rebranded naptime.* I gave it a new name, a sparkly new logo, a whole new elevator pitch. Moving forward, naptime would be known as Quiet Time.

Every day, I started putting the baby gate on the doorframe of Everett's bedroom. I'd turn on all the lights, crank up a kid-friendly playlist,

RACHEL MARIE KANG

WRITER, POET, PHOTOGRAPHER,
GRAPHIC DESIGNER, MUSICIAN, PAINTER
@RACHELMARIEKANG
CHARLOTTE, NORTH CAROLINA

Q: Why do you create?
A: I create for repair—both in myself and in the world. I believe that acts of creativity have the propensity to shine light in the darkness. Art, by any measure, can bring about laughter, beauty, truth, hope, and love—just to name a few.

Q: Do you believe everyone is creative?
A: Sometimes, I think we get caught up in the term *creative*. More than believing everyone is creative, I believe that everyone is always creating something. A painting, a meal, a picture of their children, a card to a grandparent. Our lungs create oxygen and our body creates blood. We are always making something.

get all his favorite toys down from the top of the closet, and leave him in there to play alone. We started at twenty minutes a day, then upped it to thirty, then forty, and so on. Eventually, we worked our way up to an hour of quiet time each day, and I hailed myself a parental genius. (Isn't it incredible how first-time moms go from clueless to expert in the span of a few years? Bless.)

Much to my delight, Everett began using his quiet time to build things. He would gather all his blocks, magnetic tiles, and Hot Wheels, then construct little creations all over the floor. He'd create castles and car washes and racetracks. One time, he even built a "Target"—an adorable nod to a place where we had already spent too much time and money during his short life. I don't know where he learned this word, but he started calling his creations *masterpieces*. Oftentimes, he would even dedicate them: "I made *this* masterpiece for Daddy, and I made *this* masterpiece for Mommy."

I became equal parts fascinated, impressed, and inspired by his creativity. At three years old, without any prompting whatsoever, Everett aspired to make order from chaos. To imagine what was possible. To take a messy pile of toys and turn it into a masterpiece.

Peering in at him from the hallway one day, I couldn't help but wonder, *Where did he learn this? Where did this desire to create come from?*

ONE OF THE FIRST THINGS WE LEARN about God in Scripture is that He created, and one of the first things we learn about ourselves is that we are made in His likeness. If God is the first artist—and we are a walking, breathing reflection of Him—this means our desire to create is *hereditary*, a fundamental imprint of His Spirit in us.

Right off the bat, God tasks mankind with taking care of the earth and naming the animals.[1] From the very beginning, God calls us to be good stewards of His creation and invites us to co-create with Him.

God filled the world with good things and calls us to do the same—to showcase hope, light, beauty, and restoration as part of the ongoing process of God's glory infusing the earth.

I'm reminded of Anne Lamott's words: "To be great, art has to point somewhere."[2]

God did not create us to be mere spectators, watching on the sidelines inhaling popcorn while He does all the work. Rather, He invites us to be *active* participants, co-laborers in making the invisible Kingdom visible. The act of creating is part of our calling as image bearers.

There is no better permission slip than this: to know and believe with your whole heart that the God who made you, the same God who designed blueprints for the galaxies and poured the foundation of the earth, designed you in His likeness, on purpose, for a purpose.

Permission to create already exists inside of you. It's running through your blood, your bones, every strand of DNA embedded in the body God made from dust. You have permission to pursue your creative gifts as a testament to who God created you to be. You have permission to make beautiful things in a broken world as a testament to God's grace mightily at work in you.

You don't need to wait another second for some metaphorical boss to show up at your front door with a permission slip to create. You can stop staring at the sky waiting for God to carve a yes in the clouds. He's already carved a yes in *you*.

EVERETT IS NOW NINE. He's swapped Magna-Tiles for LEGOs, and I no longer barricade him in his room for an hour a day. But his desire to create? It's still there, strong as ever. A few weeks ago, he created a "squirrel trap" in the backyard. I was slightly horrified when he told me, until I realized what he had *actually* made was more of a feeding trough. He had filled a basket with oranges from the neighbor's tree,

> Permission to create already exists inside of you. It's running through your blood, your bones, every strand of DNA embedded in the body God made from dust.

along with a handful of trail mix and a small bowl of peanut butter. Then, using a bungee cord he found in the yard, he hung the basket from a tree branch and built a set of brick "stairs" for the squirrels to reach it.

Aside from making him promise to put that bowl straight in the dishwasher when all was said and done, I blessed him on his adventures and went back to folding laundry. That day, though, I realized my kids never ask permission to create. Every day, they simply gather what's in front of them and begin making stuff: puppet shows and origami, domino towers and squirrel traps. I don't know if it's ever occurred to my children to ask whether or not they *could* create, whether or not they are *allowed to*. For them, the act of creating is a given, a birthright. Anything in this house, this garage, this yard, is fair game for masterpiece-building.

And so it is with us.

How many times do we hand our children blocks, Play-Doh, crayons, and tell them to go nuts? *Here, kids, go make something.*

Just like our children, we, too, are surrounded by raw materials brimming with possibility. God's given us the earth so we can garden. He's given us words and language so we can tell stories and record miracles. He's given us heat and metal and elements that bend so we can shape things with our hands. He's given us light, color, texture, food, music, senses that engage and make us feel alive.

Here, kids, go make something.

WHEN MY FRIEND CALLIE was struggling with whether or not to pursue her MFA as a mom of two young girls, her husband said, "Callie, you will *always* be a mom. You are not *only* a mom."

As mothers, we can be prone to feelings of guilt anytime we pursue something that takes away time from our children, especially if we deem that thing frivolous or unnecessary. Sadly, creativity is often viewed through a lens of unimportance because in our society, art rarely has value unless an audience applauds it or offers to buy it. When our creative efforts fail to yield standing ovations or impressive paychecks, it's easy to slide creativity into the hobby category, filing it away as nonessential, insignificant, or trivial.

Perhaps even . . . *selfish*.

When we label creativity as selfish, it's understandable that we'd feel immediate tension with the selflessness we typically attribute to motherhood.

Jonathan Rogers, author and creative writing teacher, addresses this specific tension in a note to mothers. He writes

> If you think of your creative efforts as primarily self-expression, or self-indulgence or self-anything, then, of course a loving, giving person is going to find it very hard to prioritize creative efforts. But I want to suggest to you that your creative efforts are among the most important ways that you can be loving and giving to your family and to the communities in which you find yourself.[3]

He goes on to reference 1 Peter 3:15, where Peter says we should always be ready to give an account of the hope that is in us. Rogers argues when we create, that is exactly what we are doing. When we engage in creative acts, when we write and draw and plant seeds in the dirt, when we create lovely things that point back to the goodness of our Maker, we are giving an account of the hope that is in us.

> Creativity is a fundamental part of being human, of being an image bearer, of being alive.

Our culture is obsessed with final products people can sell and rate, but creativity is so much more than that. Creativity is joy, and healing, and worship, the lavish combination of consciousness, gratitude, and inspiration. Creativity is not a simple commodity, something we shuffle around buying and selling at the market square. Creativity is a fundamental part of being human, of being an image bearer, of being alive.

I once heard someone describe good instructors as those who bring oxygen into a room.[4] I love that phrase, and I believe it applies to artists as well. When we make art, we bring oxygen into the room. We give people something true and beautiful to breathe in.

What if we stopped viewing creativity as something that *takes away* from our families and viewed it as something that *breathes life* into our families instead—through the meals we make, the pictures we take, the homes we decorate, the music we play, the stories we write, the gardens we grow?

What if, instead of deeming creativity as trivial or selfish, we viewed our personal creativity as a gift, an offering, a contribution capable of blessing everyone around us?

A FEW WEEKS AGO, my son came in from the backyard with a heart-shaped rock in his hand. "Look what I found!" he said, placing it on the corner of my desk. He told me it seemed like something I would like. He was right, of course. My kids notice when a cloud is shaped like a rhinoceros, or when a sunset looks like God painted the sky.

They follow my lead when I walk around our yard trimming flowers to bring inside the house, plucking their own tiny yellow buds from the grass and leaving them on my nightstand.

It's possible they would do all of this anyway, regardless of me. But I believe when we engage in the act of creating in front of our children—when we write stories and bake cookies and dig our hands in the dirt—we invite our kids to do the same. When we pay attention to the world, to the flowers growing in the cracks of sidewalks, we model an appreciation for beauty, for creation. When we walk confidently in the talents God has given us, we model faithfulness, obedience, and stewardship.

As a mother, I *want* my kids to engage in creative acts, and not just when they're little as a way to keep them occupied, or when they're teenagers as a way to keep them out of trouble. Rather, I want my children to pursue creativity for their whole lives, for the sake of the sheer joy and reverence that accompanies co-creating with their Maker.

Like anything else, if we want to instill a love of creativity in our children for the long haul, we have to model what that looks like. We have to show our kids that grown-ups are creative, too.

That *mothers* are creative, too.

You and I have been commissioned to create from the very start, by an infinitely creative God. Our permission has already been granted. We can stop waiting, hesitating, wondering if we are allowed to mother *and* create.

The answer is yes.

Let's sweep the fancy decor off the dining room table, and take our seats.

CREATIVE EXERCISE

If someone were to give you a glass jar full of permission slips you could use at any time, what would be written on them? Write a list of permission slips you can use as you mother and create.

JOURNALING PROMPT

Do you view creativity as a selfish act? Why or why not?

2

YOU HAVE EVERYTHING YOU NEED

The wall of pacifiers did me in.

Up until that point, Brett and I had skated through the aisles of the baby store with relative confidence, armed with their in-store registry app and half a dozen emails from friends listing their top five product recommendations.

We scanned everything from diapers and burp cloths to the much-raved-about Boppy pillow and Chicco KeyFit car seat. A lot of the items seemed low stakes—baby nail clippers, hooded bath towels, a sturdy diaper pail—but other products gave us pause. Surely if we registered for the right crib mattress, the right swaddle, and the right sound machine, our baby would sleep well, right? Surely if we registered for the top-rated breast pump and the perfect bottles, our baby would eat well, yes?

Surely if we registered for the *best* pacifier, our baby wouldn't cry too much?

I still remember turning the corner in the baby store and seeing the wall of pacifiers for the first time. Latex. Silicone. Orthodontic. One touted "Hospital's Choice" on the package. One glowed in the dark, making it easier to find in the middle of the night. One came with a stuffed animal attached. One proclaimed it was "modeled after Mom's nipple, but won't cause nipple confusion." I contemplated Googling "nipple confusion"—a phrase foreign to me at the time—but didn't want those words forever logged in my Internet history.

Brett wandered over to the adjacent baby monitors while I consulted my inbox, skimming every email from my friends. Not one person had recommended a pacifier. *How is that possible?* Panic set in as I stared at the fifty options in front of me. How could I make such an impossible decision on my own?

Which one of these pacifiers would comfort my baby best?

Which one of these pacifiers would make me a good mom?

ROUGHLY TWELVE YEARS AGO, I taught myself photography. Armed with a fancy hand-me-down DSLR camera my mom had purchased at Costco, I read the instruction manual from start to finish, trying to understand terms like aperture and shutter speed and ISO. Sitting on the floor of my bedroom, I played with the dials to see what they did, like a toddler pushing buttons on the TV remote. I read online articles and watched YouTube videos, Googling my way through tutorials with equal parts optimism and enthusiasm.

I rated my initial pictures as "good," certainly an improvement from the pictures I took with my phone, but not "great." Before I had even mastered the settings on the camera, I decided what I *really* needed was a better lens. If I was going to take myself seriously as a photographer, surely I needed better equipment.

After hours of poring over online reviews, I finally settled on the much-raved-about "nifty fifty" 50mm lens. My pictures improved

Which one of these pacifiers would make me a good mom?

immediately, just as the Internet assured me they would, but some of my images still appeared out of focus or overexposed. Back to the Internet I went, diving into more forums, more websites, more product reviews. Another trip to Amazon, another click-to-add-to-cart, $200 and two days later, I added a shiny new 35mm lens to my collection.

When *that* lens didn't magically fix all of my issues overnight, I wondered if perhaps my editing software was to blame.

(Dear reader, are you seeing a trend here?)

Up until that point, I had been using a free online photo editor, but I knew professional photographers used professional software. Ever convinced I was just a hop, skip, and jump (see: purchase) away from becoming A Real Photographer, I bought Lightroom. And when the basic Lightroom features failed to make my photos perfect, I bought presets. Tons and tons and *tons* of presets.

Then I bought a tripod. A reflector. A dust pen to clean my lenses. I bought a fancy padded bag, along with a leather strap to wear my camera around my neck.

I became so consumed with buying All The Right Things, the right parts, the right accessories, that I couldn't even see the real problem: I was spending more time reading Amazon reviews than taking pictures.

"DO YOU HAVE ANY BABY REGISTRY RECOMMENDATIONS?"

I'm with a friend I haven't seen in ages who hired me to take maternity photos of her. We're at a local flower farm, walking to the next photographic spot, when she confesses feeling overwhelmed by all the baby products.

I nod knowingly, recalling The Wall Of Pacifiers. Even though it's been a decade since Brett and I first walked the aisles of that baby store, I can transport myself to that moment in an instant. I remember feeling like we had just landed on the moon. *How does gravity work here?*

As my friend and I continue walking, I struggle to answer her question. What should she register for? What does she *really* need? I usually tell anyone who will listen how much we love our sound machine (we have one in every bedroom). I'm quick to recommend the swaddles that Velcro, not the blankets. When it comes to carriers, I prefer the wraps to the slings.

But every mom is different, and every baby is different, too. My first two kids never even took a pacifier (after all that drama in the baby store, can you believe it?!), but my third sleeps with hers every night. I don't care what the dentist says—she can take that thing to college for all I care. She sleeps better than any of us, and I don't believe it's a coincidence.

As I build a mental catalog of items we've loved and used, a new answer starts to bubble up inside my chest. What I wish someone had told me back then, and what I really want to tell this pregnant friend of mine now, is this: *you have everything you need.*

You have faith. You have love. These are the things that will save you in your time of need as a new mother: grace, humility, and prayer. You are already connected to the Source of abundant new mercies every morning. And on those awful, desperate days—when you need someone to pick you up off the floor, when you need something to cling to, when you need help—nothing on your baby registry is going to save you.

When your baby is cutting teeth for the first time, the best pacifier in the world is no match for your own two arms in the middle of the night. The best baby soap on the planet is not going to wash away the guilt and shame you feel after you've lost your patience for the forty-seventh time.

> When you need something to cling to,
> when you need help—nothing on your
> baby registry is going to save you.

You desperately want all the right tools because you want to mother "the right way." But motherhood is messy, and raw, and nuanced, and requires things a baby registry could never provide: surrender, and trust, and dependence on the Lord Almighty to fuel you with grace, with perseverance, with steadfast love, with a sacrificial willingness to get up the next morning with your eyes half shut and do it all over again.

That is what you need to mother.

And they don't sell it at Babies R Us.

WHEN I FIRST STARTED WRITING THIS BOOK, feeling both intimidated and daunted by the task, I signed up for a fancy word-processing program for authors. I watched the tutorial video with a glimmer of hope in my eyes, convinced I had discovered the ticket to writing a book: purchasing legitimate software to log my words and keep them organized.

Are you ready for my review?

I never made it past the thirty-day trial.

That has nothing to do with the software and everything to do with me. Because I realized, mere days into sitting down to write, my current (free) online system would serve me just fine.

A few months later, while I was in the thick of crafting my book proposal, a friend of mine announced she had applied to graduate school. She wanted to pursue an MFA in creative writing. Doubt and insecurity immediately coursed through my veins as I listened to her talk.

Do I need an MFA, too?

LAURA LAWSON VISCONTI

PAINTER, PHOTOGRAPHER
@LAURALAWSONVISCONTI
TRUCKEE, CALIFORNIA

Q: Have you ever wanted to give up or quit your creative work altogether? What kept you going?

A: When I was in college studying painting, I was diagnosed with a rare eye disease called retinitis pigmentosa, a degenerative condition that is slowly rendering me blind. I couldn't get the word *blind* out of my head, and it seemed foolish (at the time) to continue to pursue a visual medium when I wouldn't be able to see someday. For a long time, I didn't paint, as it was too painful a reminder of what was happening in my eyes. This led to an unexpected blessing: I discovered how to be creative in completely different ways. Photography and writing became new obsessions, and in time, I turned back to painting, too. Today, I'm able to dip into a palette of varying tools of self-expression to not only help me cope when the vision loss is especially taxing, but also to praise my Creator and exude joy daily.

Q: What do you want your kids to know about your creative work?

A: When I was nine months pregnant with my first baby, I decided to paint a mural on her nursery wall. The mural was 8' x 11', and with my limited dexterity, this was no small task. I want to forever remember what this felt like—to be hunched over my paint and brushes for

I spent the following afternoon researching online programs, doing math in my head, trying to figure out how I could pursue a formal writing education without putting my family in debt for a decade. Hours later, I shut my laptop in discouragement, convinced all of it remained out of reach: the financial cost, the time commitment, the emotional investment. As I cleaned up my desk for the day, cluttered

hours on end while praying over my baby in my belly as she responded with kicks and Braxton Hicks con-tractions. I had never painted a mural before. I can't wait to tell her someday that her very existence inspired me creatively in a way I'd never experienced before and gave me a reason to do something brand-new.

with notebooks and multicolored index cards, a quiet inner voice re-minded me: *you have everything you need.*

How quickly I fall into this trap. I'm right back there on the floor of my bedroom, buying photography gadgets instead of taking pictures. Spending an entire afternoon researching MFA programs instead of writing. I'm hunting, always, for the golden ticket. Where can I click *add to cart*, and check out? As if—poof!—the second the receipt shows up in my inbox, I'll be free to create. Because then I'll have everything I need.

Eventually I had to ask myself: do I *need* formal training and a framed degree hanging on my wall in order to write stories and share them with the world? While MFA programs have certainly served many writers well, do I, Ashlee Gadd, need to spend tens of thousands of dollars to validate the creative gifts God has already sewn into my heart? Or is it possible to pursue those creative gifts with what I already have, which is a compilation of forty-two messy online documents and a willingness to keep showing up to a blank page every morning at 5:30 a.m. asking God to meet me on the page?

Is that . . . *enough*?

THERE'S A PASSAGE I LOVE IN LUKE 9, where Jesus calls the disciples and sends them off to preach the Good News and heal the sick. His next direction, however, is downright shocking: "Take nothing for your journey, no staff, nor bag, nor bread, nor money; and do not have two tunics."[1]

I don't know about you, but if I'm a disciple at this moment, I think I'd be scratching my head. *Not even an outfit change, Lord? Jesus, are you serious? Surely we need a backpack? A pocketknife? A fishing net? A cute-but-practical pair of shoes?*

But no. Jesus tells them to take nothing.

The disciples didn't need fancy belongings or supplies to preach the gospel. They needed *faith.* Traveling light ensured the disciples would stay dependent on God throughout their journey. They'd need to rely on Him for food, for water, for housing, for everything. This profound trust and whole dependence on God not only carried the disciples through their quest, it also became part of their testimony.

How can we live like this as mothers? As artists?

What do we actually *need* to write, to take pictures, to garden?

When we spend all of our hours and all of our money investing in the right "supplies" to mother and create, we can easily lose sight of the tools God has already provided us. We quickly forget that "we are God's handiwork, created in Christ Jesus to do good works, which God prepared in advance for us to do."[2]

What do we actually *need* to write, to take pictures, to garden? What do we need to sew, to play music, to make pottery? Our creative work will require some essentials, of course, but before we go crazy with those online shopping carts, and before we take out a loan for grad school on a whim, let's take inventory of what we already have. We have God-ordained creativity flowing inside of us. We have palms willing to open in surrender, hearts willing to obey when called. We have trust in an artistic God who has equipped us with curiosity, wonder, the perseverance to fail and try again. We have the humility to ask God for what we lack, along with the faith that He will provide.

We are wholly equipped to pursue the creative dreams stirring in our hearts, not because we dropped $200 on new supplies, but because God has already planted passion, endurance, imagination, and artistry in our bones. We are wholly equipped to love our children, not because we chose the right pacifier, but because the ability to love and comfort and nurture is wired into our DNA by the same God who loves and comforts and nurtures us.

God loves His children; therefore, we love ours. God created; therefore, we create. Every good thing we know how to do, we know because we first experienced it by His hand.

We already have everything we need.

SPINE POETRY

Take a look at your bookshelves and grab every title
that appeals to you. Play around with the words and
phrases, stacking the books on top of one another to
make a poem.

She dreams

(of) room to write,

inspired,

wild words,

searching for God knows what—

glimmers of hope,

the march of faith.

Am I there yet?

Falling free,

fighting forward,

still writing—

the magic of motherhood

a million little ways.

It's what I do.

CREATIVE EXERCISE

Walk around your house and take inventory of creative supplies you've purchased and never used. Do you have notebooks collecting dust in a drawer somewhere? Seed packets you picked up and never planted? A cookbook you've never opened or tried? Dream a little— can you set aside some intentional time this week to put any of those supplies to use?

JOURNALING PROMPT

With your specific creative gifting in mind, make one list of what you need, and one list of what you already have. Consider tangible supplies as well as character traits, attitudes, perspectives, etc. Comparing the lists, what do you notice?

3

READY OR NOT

Moments before we learn we are going to become parents, Brett and I are standing at the foot of the bed folding laundry as I casually mention today is the day. One pregnancy test and we'd know for sure.

He drops the towel in his hand.

"Are you serious? What are you waiting for? Go take the test!" he says, pushing me toward the bathroom. I freeze.

"Let's finish folding these towels first," I tell him, trying my best to remain calm. The room suddenly feels ten degrees warmer.

We continue folding towels in silence, while my heart pounds against my T-shirt. I seem to be folding in slow motion, as if three extra minutes will buy me the time I need to wrap my head around the possibility that my entire life is about to change.

Brett sets the last folded towel on the stack and looks at me expectantly.

I feel like I am going to be sick.

Why do I feel so panicked right now? Why don't I feel . . . ready?

I have wanted to be a mom since I was eight years old, back when I used to swaddle Kimber, my plastic baby doll, before gently tucking her under my floral bedspread for one of her seventeen daily naps. Brett and I talked about kids on our first date. I wanted two, he was open to more. After only a few months of dating, we started discussing baby names, just for fun.

On our second wedding anniversary, we wrote down a list of fifteen things we wanted to do before embarking upon parenthood. We called it The Pre-Baby Bucket List.

Over the next few years, we slowly crossed items off the list as we could afford to do so. We flew to Los Angeles for a taping of *The Tonight Show*, where I managed to sweet-talk the staff into letting us keep one of Conan O'Brien's cue cards as a souvenir. At a local cooking class, we learned how to make homemade pasta (which confirmed what we already knew: we are store-bought pasta type of people). We took a road trip to Oregon, fueled eight hours each way by gas station snacks, cold bottles of Diet Dr Pepper, and an epic playlist. We learned how to make apple strudel with his grandmother, and chocolate fudge with mine.

In the spring of 2011, we crossed the number one item off our list: a trip to Greece. After reading hundreds of TripAdvisor reviews and setting aside money from every paycheck for nearly two years, my passport finally received its first stamp.

Stepping off the plane in Santorini felt like stepping into a postcard.

On our second night in Oia, we ran to the tip of the island to watch the sunset. By the time we reached the overlook, a huge crowd had gathered. People stood lined up against the edge of the cliff on various levels and steps, cameras dutifully in hand. We finally found a pocket of space and wedged ourselves in between a handful of tourists. Once the very top of the sun disappeared into the water, the entire crowd around us began cheering. We cheered with them, clapping and screaming as if the sun itself could hear us and was contemplating an encore performance.

This was the moment we had waited for, the grand finale of the pre-baby bucket list. We were ready to start a family.

Or so I thought.

But here we are, months later, staring at two pink lines in disbelief. Brett picks me up in the air and twirls me around on the bedroom carpet, smiling and laughing. I'm smiling, too. But my excitement starts to wane as panic shows up in its place.

How painful is birth?

What if the baby never sleeps?

What do we even know about raising children?

I'm not ready for this.

THREE YEARS LATER, on a balmy summer night, another baby takes up space in my body while a humming laptop warms my legs. I've just polished off a small bag of Cheetos, my pregnancy snack of choice, and am trying—unsuccessfully—to blow orange crumbs off my keyboard.

After eight months of praying, planning, and teaching myself how to build a website, I schedule the first post to be published on Coffee + Crumbs: a new collaborative blog where mothers can share honest stories with each other.

I schedule the post to go live the following morning and whisper a prayer before bed as the baby in my belly does a series of cartwheels. *God, do whatever you want with this.*

Over the next six weeks, my little "passion project" receives more than two million pageviews after some of the content goes viral. My inbox fills up with a hundred emails. *Love the site! Can I write for you? Can we republish this essay?*

Friends and family members alike send congratulatory texts, thrilled for my rapid success. *Just saw your piece in the* Huffington Post! *Remember me when you're famous!*

In a span of three months, Coffee + Crumbs unexpectedly morphs from a hobby into a full-time job. Suddenly my days consist of scrolling emails and texts on the bathroom floor, where I sit propped up against the bathtub, coaxing my reluctant potty-training toddler onto the toilet with a newborn attached to my boob. After wiping a glob of spit-up out of my bra and helping my toddler into a fresh pull-up, I wonder what I've just gotten myself into.

I'm not ready for this.

I GOT MARRIED AT TWENTY-ONE YEARS OLD, in between my junior and senior year of college. Most of my friends who married young attended small Christian colleges, but I attended a public university where I became known as The Married Girl, something of an anomaly. I remember sitting in the student union one day when a girl from one of my communication classes asked me skeptically, "How did you know you were *ready* to get married?"

I don't remember how I answered her then, but if I had to answer her now, I think I'd simply say, "I don't know. We took a leap of faith."

Like many other couples, our first year of marriage brought about its fair share of challenges, conflict, and shattered expectations. Looking back, it would be easy to wonder if we simply weren't ready for marriage. Perhaps we should have gone to more premarital counseling, completed more worksheets, spent more time discussing budgeting and chores and sex *before* walking down the aisle.

I don't know, though. If we could go back in time and log more hours preparing ourselves for marriage, would the extra homework have made a difference? Are you ever truly ready to commit your life to someone? Or does marriage, as with most big scary things, ultimately boil down to a leap of faith?

Most of us want to feel ready before embarking upon marriage, or motherhood, or a big creative dream. We want to feel equipped, qualified, as prepared as a Girl Scout. We're often tempted to believe that if we just plot and plan enough, if we make enough lists and spreadsheets, if we take enough classes and read enough books, one day we'll wake up and all of our fears will float away into the sky, like a bouquet of helium balloons slipping through the grasp of a toddler's hand.

But what if that day never comes?

What if we never feel ready to walk down the aisle, or see those two pink lines on a pregnancy test, or submit the adoption paperwork? What if we never feel ready to hit "publish" on that first blog post, or say yes to participating in that art show? What if we never feel ready to release our ideas, our dreams, our masterpieces into the world?

Despite wanting to be a mom my entire life, I still did not feel ready to see two lines on that first pregnancy test. The night before my scheduled C-section, even after nine whole months of anticipation, I broke down sobbing in the bathroom while brushing my teeth. I didn't feel ready to give birth. I didn't feel ready to relinquish the romance and freedom of our sweet married life.

I didn't feel ready to be a mother at all.

The next morning, after hours of fasting and praying, I remained perfectly still on a metal table under fluorescent lights as a team of doctors carefully sliced open my body and asked if I was ready to meet my son.

I nodded yes from my side of the curtain, which seemed like the only appropriate answer.

Minutes later, they placed a slippery blue-eyed baby boy on my chest, and fresh tears streamed down my face.

Ready or not, there he was.

"THIS IS FUN, BUT TERRIFYING!"

That blue-eyed baby is now nine years old, gripping a wobbly rope while stepping across even wobblier wooden planks. We are twenty-something feet in the air, walking from treetop to treetop across an obstacle course that seems more suitable for squirrels than human beings. I follow my son across the teetering steps with shaking legs.

"Whatever you do," he shouts with a smile from the platform, "DON'T LOOK DOWN!"

Two and a half hours later, we finish the course. My hands are numb and my legs are burning, and all I can think about is stopping at In-N-Out for a well-deserved burger and fries on the way home. I barely get out the word *milkshake* before Everett lights up in agreement.

> At the root, my desire to feel ready is actually a desire to control the outcome.

On our way to the parking lot, we pass the most difficult course, which is perched considerably higher in the trees than the one we've just completed. As we watch a few kids make their way across rickety steps high above our heads, Everett wonders out loud if anyone has ever fallen from the course. I assure him the answer is no, but I can tell he doesn't believe me.

"Ask Nico," I urge him, nodding my head toward the guide walking behind us.

"What's up, bud?" Nico asks.

Everett practically whispers, "Has anyone ever . . . *fallen?*"

"Into their harness? Sure," Nico responds.

Sensing he didn't ask the right question, Everett clarifies, "No, I mean . . . has anyone ever fallen to the *ground?*"

Nico smiles. "Never."

Everett's shoulders relax into his body. "Man! I wish I had known that all along! Next time we come here, I'm going to RUN across that course," he tells me.

I chuckle at his newfound confidence, knowing full well that trusting your harness doesn't automatically cure a fear of heights.

NINE YEARS INTO MOTHERHOOD, I still don't feel qualified for this work. Just last week, Everett told us a boy and girl in his class are "boyfriend and girlfriend." My exact words? *I'm not ready for this.*

I keep waiting for that magical moment when I am finally going to feel settled, confident, fully and totally capable of raising these children. Most days I still feel like a child myself, peering over my

shoulder wondering when the Real Adult is going to swoop in and take over. Sometimes I feel like I'm twenty years old and someone just handed me three kids and ran away. This feeling of *not being ready* seems to be a perpetual, inescapable state of motherhood for me. It just takes on different shapes as my kids get older.

I feel the same way about my art. You'd think after writing on the Internet for twelve years and publicly pursuing a number of creative endeavors, I'd feel equipped to tackle whatever idea flies into my brain next. In reality, I am sweating and taking deep breaths, nervous and insecure, pondering all the what-ifs.

What if I launch a newsletter and people unsubscribe? What if I submit my writing and it gets rejected? What if I get a one-star review on Amazon? And iTunes? And all the other places people can publicly rate my work? What if I publish this vulnerable blog post and someone misunderstands what I am trying to say? What if I mess up? What if I fail?

At the root, my desire to feel ready is actually a desire to control the outcome. I want to be adequately prepared for every possible result *before* I take the leap.

But that's not faith, is it?

God continues to call me out of my comfort zone, like when He nudges me to explore a new art form, or share something vulnerable I've written, or speak on a stage even though I hate public speaking. Like Peter being beckoned to join Jesus on the water, I always have a choice to make. I can move toward Him, or I can stay in the boat.

Maybe you're afraid to begin at all, because deep down inside, you don't actually believe you are creative. Or maybe you're afraid of failing. Maybe you're afraid people will laugh at you, or judge you, or make fun of you behind your back. Maybe you're afraid of bad reviews. Maybe you're afraid of rejection, or afraid you're going to invest time and money into a creative dream that never reaps a monetary reward. Maybe you're afraid nobody will support you, and that you're just going to embarrass yourself.

Here's something that might make you feel better. All of my what-ifs? *They actually happened.* I did start a newsletter, and every single time I send one out, people unsubscribe. I've submitted my writing and been rejected. Even better, I've *paid* to submit my writing and been rejected. I have received one-star reviews on both Amazon and iTunes, and probably other places I don't even know about, in addition to dozens of emails over the years that are basically a one-star review of both my character and creative work (always a delight!). I have been misunderstood. I have invested money and time into creative endeavors that have unequivocally failed.

I say this not to scare you, but to offer a testimony. When all of those bad things happened—rejection and criticism and failure—the reality turned out to be far less scary than the picture I had painted in my head.

Last year I spoke with a friend who had recently weathered a storm in her creative work. She hosts a well-known and well-loved podcast, but one of her episodes had unexpectedly garnered a lot of negative feedback. She ended up pulling the episode down, making a public apology, the whole thing. I had no idea this had happened. I was shocked.

I'm so sorry, I told her over and over.

I will never forget her response. She shrugged and smiled and told me, in a way, she was glad it happened.

"Don't get me wrong—it was terrible dealing with all of that," she said, "but the whole situation wasn't as bad as I thought it would be. God carried us through."

Criticism did not end her creativity; it was merely a pothole in the road.

My friend went on to say she had always considered "public backlash" to be a terrifying what-if scenario. But when the public backlash *actually* happened, and she realized she was okay, that hypothetical what-if didn't seem so scary anymore.

Both motherhood and creativity involve risk and require courage. We might never feel ready or prepared, but that's where the leap of faith comes in.

I nodded. It's kind of like losing your balance on the treetop course and realizing you only fell two feet into your harness. You're still safe. You can get back up, dust yourself off. My friend could have made a choice to quit right then and there in the midst of all that negative feedback. Instead, she kept going. She kept creating anyway, getting out of the boat, making a beautiful podcast that encourages and equips thousands of women each week.

Both motherhood and creativity involve risk and require courage. We might never feel ready or prepared, but that's where the leap of faith comes in. And here's some good news: God loves to use unqualified people. As Madeleine L'Engle writes in *Walking on Water*:

> God continually chooses the most unqualified to do his work, to bear his glory. If we are qualified, we tend to think that we have done the job ourselves. If we are forced to accept our evident lack of qualification, then there's no danger that we will confuse God's work with our own, or God's glory with our own.[1]

Accepting that we are unqualified and unready feels a lot like approaching the treetop course with wobbly legs, but a heart that trusts the safety harness. It's a sense of security, of knowing that even if we fall off the rope, we're not going to fall to the ground.

I know your knees are shaking. Mine are, too. I know you can still feel your heart beating through your T-shirt. I can feel mine, too. But I'm starting to think this is normal, and good, and maybe even a little bit holy. Maybe one of the best things we can do is learn to get comfortable with the butterflies in our stomachs. Maybe one of the best things we can do is embrace the idea that we are unqualified, because then we leave room for a bigger leap of faith.

It's time to get out of the boat.

Ready or not, here we go.

CREATIVE EXERCISE

Make a list of creative dreams stirring in your heart right now. Practice saying them out loud. What is one concrete step you could take this week toward one of those dreams?

JOURNALING PROMPT

Write down every fear you have surrounding your creativity, an unfiltered list of every what-if. Then consider—have you ever experienced a "harness moment" where you stumbled, but looking back, you can see now how God caught you?

4

MAKING SPACE

I am standing in line at Panera, eight months pregnant, craving every single thing on the menu. When the young, pretty cashier asks what I'd like on the side of my turkey sandwich, I whisper, "Bread."

If she judges me for ordering bread on the side of a sandwich, she hides it well. I order everything to go because even in my obvious pregnant state, I am slightly embarrassed by the amount of carbs I plan to consume in a single sitting.

A few minutes later, paper bag in hand and the taste of sourdough practically on my tongue, I approach my car in the parking lot, only to discover there is another vehicle parked inconsiderately close to mine. I fish keys out of my purse, unlock the doors, and attempt to shimmy myself in between the two cars. It takes exactly two seconds to realize I do not fit. I cannot open the car door wide enough to accommodate my eight-month-pregnant belly.

There isn't enough space.

I stand there for a minute, sweating in the sun, contemplating my options. *Should I wait for the owner to return? How long will that take?*

Should I go back into Panera and have the staff blast the license plate number over the loudspeaker?

The wafting scent of sourdough pushes me over the edge, leading me to do what any other pregnant lady would (probably?) do in that situation.

I climb through the passenger door and twist my body over the center console, as ungracefully as one can possibly imagine, grunting like a hog, into my driver's seat.

As I awkwardly twist my legs down under the steering wheel and push strands of hair off my sweaty forehead, I realize a number of people sitting on the Panera patio are watching this scene unfold with looks of amusement on their faces. After they enjoy a front row seat to the circus show, I half expect them to applaud the pregnant lady's impressive trick. (No one does. *Rude.*) My face burns with embarrassment and I quickly back out of the parking spot.

At the first red light, I open that glorious bag. I drive home with one hand on the steering wheel and the other shoving a piece of bread into my mouth.

DID YOU KNOW WHEN A WOMAN IS PREGNANT, her organs rearrange themselves inside her body to make space for her baby?

In the fall of 2011, right around the time my organs started playing their first game of Tetris, I pushed aside the trendy, stylish clothes hanging in my closet to make room for maternity jeans and flattering potato sacks. Baby bottles and breast pump accessories took over the kitchen cabinets, while various forms of nipple cream took up residence in the bathroom drawers. I moved small pieces of furniture around the living room to make space for a swing and a Bumbo and one of those little activity mats with the Velcro attachments. Then there was the matter of a bassinet, a stroller, an obnoxiously bright ExerSaucer we borrowed from a friend.

Already somewhat of a self-proclaimed minimalist, I remember standing in my house one day staring at all the stuff, hands on my hips, thinking, *Wow, babies take up a lot of space.*

First, my body. Then, the house. Finally, when the baby arrived, any remnants of free space residing in my brain vanished. New motherhood propelled me into a foreign, all-consuming inner dialogue: *Is the bathwater too hot? Did he hear that bad word on the TV? What is this rash and how do I get rid of it, and will his hair ever grow in on the top?*

Nine years and two more babies later, these children I love beyond measure have inundated every single aspect of my home, my schedule, my heart, and my mind. They've taken over my life, parked themselves in my lap, and planted a flag. They've marked me as their territory.

(Literally. These kids have peed on me more times than I can count.)

Every time I turn around, there they are. Their needs are great. Their requests are plentiful. Their LEGOs and empty applesauce

pouches are everywhere. *How are they already hungry again? Why can't anyone find their socks?* Everett needs help with his homework. Carson needs a cotton ball for an art project. Presley is outside by herself, scooping up dirt with a shovel and dumping it in her shoes. Most days, my house sounds like a cross between a toddler rave and a pet store. One minute my kids will be dancing to "Baby Shark" on full volume, the next they're pretending to be puppies, barking and panting at one another in the grass.

I don't know who invented noise canceling headphones, but I'd like to think it was a mom.

Mothers balance a lot—we're working, we're tending to marriages and friendships, we're getting the kids to school in (mostly) clean underwear, we're putting some form of dinner on the table, we're keeping the house stocked with toothpaste and diapers. We're singing songs and boiling pasta and meeting deadlines and remembering to return the library books.

Sometimes it feels impossible to simply go to the bathroom or eat a hot meal without an interruption. We desire a clutter-free zone to focus on our art, but no matter where we turn, the Hot Wheels are procreating, along with traces of crusty Play-Doh. (Do not even get me started on glitter.) Sometimes we wish our minds could hold more than appointments, grocery lists, birthday party RSVPs, and a detailed log of which children have outgrown their pajamas.

Since becoming a mother, I've often felt like Gumby, pulled in opposite directions, trying to figure out how to be everywhere and do everything, stretching myself thin in the process.

In busy seasons and times of stress, I'm back to fantasizing about that elusive cabin in the woods. I'm back to believing if I just had a little more space, and a little more time, *then* I could create. If I only had a workspace, and all my kids in school, *then* I could make my creative dreams come true. It's simple, really. All I need is a room of my own

PLACES I'VE WRITTEN

On the bathroom floor, next to my daughter in the tub

On the sidelines of soccer practice, sitting in the grass

At the dining room table, surrounded by crumbs

In my bed

In the Target parking lot

On the living room floor, surrounded by LEGOs

At the kitchen counter

Sitting in my car in the driveway

In the waiting room at the doctor's office

On a lawn chair in my backyard

Next to the pool at the gym

At the beach

On an airplane

In many freezing cold coffee shops

In the rocking chair, while I nurse a baby to sleep

During church (don't tell anyone)

In the shower, in my head

YOUR TURN

_____

_____

with soundproof walls, cold brew coffee on tap, and hours and hours of affordable childcare.

Is that really too much to ask?

YOU MAY RECALL I started writing this book on index cards, sitting on the bathroom floor. My writing environment didn't exactly improve after that. I finished writing the first two chapters in my car, during a global pandemic.

If you're picturing me parked at some scenic overlook, staring off at a lake or ocean, drawing poetic inspiration from the view, let me stop you right there. The two places I wrote in my car were my own drive-way and the Starbucks parking lot.

Perspective is everything, though, because a couple of months into the pandemic, my mobile office became somewhat of a sanctuary. When my childcare disappeared overnight and all of the coffee shops and libraries shut their doors, I had to get creative. So every afternoon, I'd put my daughter down for her nap, set my boys up with something to do, and then grab a bubbly water from the fridge and stroll out to my car with my book, journal, and laptop in tow. Occasionally I'd leave the kids home with Brett and venture down the street to the Starbucks drive-thru, which thankfully stayed open. I'd order a decaf almond milk mocha and pull the car around to a front parking spot where I could still access the Wi-Fi. After turning the car off, I'd exit the driver's door and reenter on the passenger side, where I could put my laptop on my legs without the nuisance of a steering wheel crowding my space.

Was I willing to fight for the very thing that helps me make sense of the world?

Around the time I started working out of my parked car, I also began setting my alarm for 5:00 a.m. Before you write me off as a morning person, let the record state: I am *not*, by nature, a morning person. In fact, I started waking up at 6:30 a.m. and gradually worked my way back in five-minute increments until I could wake up at 5:00 a.m. without groaning at the sound of that wretched alarm.

In that exhausting, confusing, grief-filled season, there were days when creating in the margins felt like an impossible, futile balancing act. With five people suddenly under our small roof 24/7, it often felt like the walls were closing in, as if our home were shrinking like a sweater left in the dryer too long. *Has everyone always chewed this loudly?*

Trying to carve out space for creativity while also scouring stores for toilet paper felt straight-up meaningless most days. *Seriously, what is the point of writing when the world is falling apart? Why am I even still trying to create?*

I could have easily given up. I had every reason to. Nobody would have noticed if I stopped creating during a pandemic. Nobody would have cared if I didn't write poetry when the world was on fire. Nobody would have noticed if I quit taking pictures, if I stopped documenting what would always be remembered as one of the strangest years of our lives.

But what about me?

Would *I* notice? Would *I* care?

Was I willing to fight for the very thing that helps me make sense of the world, the practice that helps me channel my angst and disappointment and heartache into something filled with purpose and beauty? Was I willing to make space for creativity in a tumultuous year filled with loss and grief—not only for the sake of my own heart and mental health—but also for the subsequent well-being of my family, who would surely be better cared for by a mother who also cared for herself?

Was I willing to create in my car?

Was I willing to get up before dawn?

Was I willing to think outside the box, to fight for the space for my own imagination to thrive even though I had no childcare and no privacy and nowhere to work?

A quiet inner voice. *Yes.*

IN HIS BOOK *CULTURE CARE,* Makoto Fujimura recounts a time when he and his wife were struggling to make ends meet. One day,

MICHELLE WINDSOR

POET
BONITA SPRINGS, FLORIDA
@MICHELLEVWINDSOR

Q: How has motherhood shaped, shifted, or changed your creative practices?
A: I didn't start writing, at least not in the way I do now, until my first son was almost two. Motherhood opened that door for me, and it was almost impossible not to walk through. I learned how to be a mother and a writer at the same time, and there are too many metaphor possibilities here, so I'll just say that motherhood and writing have made me question everything I thought I knew about myself and helped me find the parts of me I didn't know existed.

There is no way to tell a woman
Standing on the edge of motherhood
What it's like to drown and fly
You can only stand with her
Offer your hand to pull her up
Help her reach the sky
        MW

much to his dismay, she brought home a bouquet of flowers. He said to her, "How could you think of buying flowers if we can't even eat!"

Her response? "We need to feed our souls, too."[1]

At the core, making space for creativity traces back to permission, to the idea that feeding our souls is not a waste. Creativity is not a waste of time, or money, or resources. It's not a waste of space in our schedules, our minds, our homes.

If you view creativity as a selfish act, you will always struggle to justify making time for it. If you believe pursuing creativity is self-serving, it's going to be the first thing you cut from your life in busy seasons.

We have to ask ourselves, over and over again: is the act of creating life-giving to us? Does pursuing creativity benefit our minds, our hearts, our souls? Zoom out. Is the art we create life-giving to others? Does the act of creating leave us more in awe of our Creator, more in tune with the Spirit moving within us? Does creating make us better women? Better mothers? Better friends? Does creativity provide us with gifts to offer back to the world?

In order to make space for creativity, we first must believe it is *worthy* of taking up space.

Carving out space to create requires imagination, innovation, and yes, sacrifice. We have to stay nimble, adaptable, ready to pounce on whatever sliver of time presents itself. We have to stay grounded in our why, our purpose, the belief that our creativity *matters*—to us, to our families, to the culture at large, and most importantly, to our Maker.

We make space for the things we love, for the things we deem essential to our own well-being. Creativity is not a luxury, or a frivolous indulgence we can easily trim from the family budget.

You may not have a room of your own. You may not have hours and hours of uninterrupted time. But what *do* you have?

You might not have much. I do not know one mother with a cabin in the woods who gets to escape every weekend to pursue her creative dreams. But moms know how to be flexible better than anyone. We know how to improvise, how to think on our feet. We know how to combine three leftover meals into a new creation and call it dinner. We know how to bathe our children with baby wipes in a pinch. We are perfectly capable of solving this Rubik's Cube.

Can you get up thirty minutes earlier? Swap an hour of scrolling social media for creating instead? Can you carve out a nook in your house? Reclaim a window seat and tuck a basket of knitting supplies in the corner? Is there a desk collecting dust somewhere, piled high with six months of junk mail? If the dining room table is your best bet, can you invest in a rolling cart to keep your art supplies nearby?

Ask yourself, *what is it going to take to make this work?*

Because every minute spent pining for that cabin in the woods is a minute lost on creating something beautiful in the actual life you are living.

FOR A LONG TIME, I held on to a specific vision of what "space" looked like for me, a mother who creates. Space looked like a pretty home office, one that belonged to me and only me. A private room where I could not, under any circumstances, hear anyone crying or fighting or breathing or chewing. It would have a large desk, tons of hanging plants, and a door that locked. Space looked like affordable childcare on demand. It looked like time in my schedule to not only create, but also to read and take solitary walks around my neighborhood, regularly carving out room to be alone with my thoughts.

My friend Anna once referred to a conversation with her husband as an "expectation management meeting." As someone prone to high expectations of myself and others and, well, just about everything, the phrase struck a chord with me.

I've been creating and mothering for nearly a decade. In that time, I've been forced to have a lot of expectation management meetings

> In order to make space for creativity, we first must believe it is *worthy* of taking up space.

with myself, usually in seasons when I am feeling disappointed and frustrated that my ideal version of space looks different than the reality. When resentment and irritation start building up inside my chest, I have to zoom out and ask myself a series of questions.

What does space look like and feel like on a normal, ordinary day, as part of my normal, ordinary life? *Where* can I create? *When* can I create? How can I make space to pursue my creativity—right here, right now—in my actual life?

What am I being called to?

What creative dreams are stirring in my heart?

Am I willing to make sacrifices? Less sleep? Less Netflix? Less Instagram?

I've had seasons when I created between eight and eleven in the evening, and others when I created every afternoon during naptime. I've had months when I had childcare available on standby, and others when I had a simple babysitting swap with a friend one morning a week. There was a short, sweet time when I had a home office to call my own, but there have been far more years where I've steadily rotated between my bed and the dining room table.

I've had to learn and relearn to set realistic expectations, to stay flexible, to roll with the punches. Out of sheer necessity, I've learned to chisel out a corner, a nook, in any room, at any time. I've learned to create sitting and standing and lying down, both away from my kids and with my kids in the room. (The noise canceling headphones help with the latter.) With practice, the sheer act of creating has become part of my daily cadence, as natural as eating and sleeping and brushing my teeth.

Some seasons, I've been able to slip into a creative routine without too much effort or commotion. Other times, I've had to carve out space with a butcher knife, cutting loose distractions and slicing free time into efficient chunks. And I think that's just the way it is, depending on the season you're in, how many kids you have, how old they are, what your daily rhythms look like.

Sometimes making space for creativity is as simple as setting the alarm a little earlier each day, hiring the neighborhood babysitter for a couple of hours, clearing clutter from an unused desk. Other times, making space for creativity looks like an eight-month pregnant lady awkwardly shoving her own gigantic body into her car through the wrong door. There's a lot of bending and grunting involved.

When we believe creativity is worthy of taking up space, we'll find a way.

CREATIVE EXERCISE

This week, find a way to reclaim some space for yourself. If you need physical space, can you reorganize and declutter a corner of your home? Or maybe it's mental space you're craving. Can you delete your social media apps for a week (or two, or three)? Take a few minutes to think about what "space" looks like in your real, *actual* life—and what that space can offer you. Then, make it so.

JOURNALING PROMPT

Do you believe creativity is worthy of taking up space in your life? Why or why not?

5

WHOSE VOICE ARE YOU LISTENING TO?

The first time I say, "I'm a writer" without stumbling over my words, I am sitting at the Asheville airport next to a nine-year-old girl named Didi.

I am heading home from a writing conference; she is flying home to her mom in Portland after visiting her dad. Both of our flights have been canceled. Didi reminds me a lot of myself at that age, nine going on nineteen. When she mentions her baby sister, I pull up a picture of Everett, who is eighteen months old. I hold the phone out in front of her face and watch her eyes light up.

"He is *soooooooooo* cute!!!"

We make small talk for a few minutes, chatting about babies and the weather and how early we both had to get up that morning. When the conversation starts to lull, I ask her: "So, what do you want to be when you grow up?"

Without missing a beat, she answers confidently, "An actress."

I smile at her the way adults used to smile at me when I offered the same answer to the same question many years ago.

"Wow," I tell her, "I wanted to be an actress, too, when I was your age."

She tilts her head to the side and looks up at me curiously, waiting for the punchline.

"But then I grew up . . ." I continue, "and I changed my mind. Now, I'm a writer."

I don't know if I'm simply feeling brave and confident after the writing conference I've just attended, or if it's the non-intimidating presence of a nine-year-old girl, but for the very first time, after years and years of stumbling over a title I've been terrified to claim, the word *writer* flows out of my mouth like honey dripping from a spoon, sweet and smooth.

"YOUR SON HAS TEMPORARY HEARING LOSS," the doctor tells us.

His tone is flat, unalarmed, as if announcing the walls are, indeed, beige. My son Everett, now three years old, is sitting on a chair next to us, oblivious, playing the Elmo ABC app on my phone.

"His ears are full of fluid," the doctor continues, pulling up a graph on his computer. "This is average hearing," he says pointing to a section toward the top, "and this is what your son can hear right now," he says, moving his finger to a dotted line at the bottom of the chart. "If an adult came in here with this level of hearing, we would recommend a hearing aid."

In a moment of irony, I am not sure I've heard the doctor correctly. My mind whirls back to scene after scene: every time Everett ignored me, every time he asked me to turn the music up louder in the car, every "Huh?" after I asked him to put away a toy.

"Kids are adaptable," the doctor reassures us with a shrug. "He probably got used to this impairment a while ago and adjusted to it. We'll put tubes in his ears, and he'll be good as new."

The doctor continues to speak directly, plainly, without an ounce of judgment in his voice, as if three-year-olds lose their hearing all the time, as if this is no big deal. He tells my husband and me what to expect at the pre-op appointment, how long the procedure will take, and what the recovery will be like.

I'm tempted to defend myself. I feel the need to explain how I, as Everett's primary caregiver, missed this "impairment." *Don't a lot of three-year-olds struggle with listening?* My friends and I are always commiserating about our kids ignoring us. We often feel like the adults in the Peanuts series, as if all our words come out as *wah wah wah* through the muted sounds of a trombone.

As the ENT doctor hands me a waiver to sign, I am transported back to every pediatrician appointment I've attended over the past three years. My mind flashes to every time I've been in the hot seat fielding a slew of questions I can't always answer. *How many ounces of breast milk is he getting per feeding? Does your baby know how to pick up a Cheerio with his thumb and finger? Does your child say at least fifteen words?*

I stammer through the questions, trying my best, before the grand finale: *Do you have poison control saved in your phone? Are your cleaning supplies locked up or placed in a high cabinet?*

I nod yes, even though the answer is no.

On the way home from the ENT's office, I turn the radio on to drown out my guilt, spinning the dial until it lands on a top-forty station. An old Eminem song is playing, "Will the real Slim Shady please stand up?"

I picture a bunch of authorities in uniforms and lab coats bursting into the doctor's office announcing the jig is up. It's official. They know I have no clue what I am doing. They can see me for who I really am: an imposter mom. My child hasn't been able to hear for who knows how long, and *I didn't even notice.* What kind of mother am I? The strangers surround me, drawing closer and closer, their lab coats creating a suffocating cloud of white fabric around my face.

Will Everett's real mom please stand up?

I repeat, will Everett's real mom please stand up?

I AM SITTING AT MY COMPUTER, candle burning, sipping a lukewarm cup of coffee I am too lazy to microwave again. My hands are positioned on the keyboard, fingers ready to move, when the voice sets in:

You're not a real writer.

Who do you think you are?

I hear it again while I'm sitting in my car, preparing to walk into a friend's house to photograph her family. I take a few deep breaths, triple-check my camera battery, make sure I have two extra memory cards on hand.

Do you even know how to use all of the settings on this camera?

You're a fraud.

It's only a matter of time before someone finally exposes me for the fraud I am.

I hear it again when I am standing off to the side in an auditorium, palms sweating, preparing to speak to a hundred mothers at a MOPS meeting.

You have nothing worthwhile to say.

You don't deserve to be here.

This voice follows me everywhere, hissing little lies into my ears like the serpent in Eden. It wraps me in self-doubt, assuring me that any minute now, someone is going to discover my talents are fake. That any success I've experienced has been a stroke of luck, and nothing more. That deep down inside, I have no idea what I'm doing, and it's only a matter of time before someone finally exposes me for the fraud I am.

I still remember driving home from the hospital with our first baby cradled in his brand-new car seat, drowning in a newborn outfit far too big for him. I rode beside Everett in the back seat, anxiety flooding me each time we bopped over a speed bump, staring at his tiny face in disbelief that we were allowed to take him home. The nurses didn't even flinch when they waved us away. *Here are your discharge papers; have a nice life!* How did we get away with it? How did we convince them we were equipped to care for this baby? It felt like a heist, like driving home in a getaway car. Nobody even asked if we knew how to heat a bottle. Two years prior, while babysitting for a friend, my husband and I put a bottle in the microwave, and it melted.

Seriously—*who let us take this baby home?!*

I feel like an imposter every time I'm at the pediatrician's office, being lectured about my baby's weight. *Tsk tsk tsk.* The doctor shakes his head, pointing to dots on a growth chart as if I'm failing a very important homework assignment. I feel like an imposter every time my toddler is throwing a tantrum in public and people are staring, surely questioning whether I am the mother or the babysitter. Don't even get me started on those comprehensive parenting forms, like the seventy-two-page preschool questionnaire that asks questions like "What is your child's blood type?" and "What is your child's personality?" and—let's not forget the most important—"What word does your child use to describe a bowel movement?"

They want ME to answer these questions?!

Will Everett's real mom please stand up?

I joined a playgroup around the time Everett turned one, and I will never forget standing in the kitchen when one of the moms asked incredulously, "Who brought the grapes? Why aren't they cut in half?"

I brought the grapes. *I* didn't know you were supposed to cut grapes in half. What kind of mom doesn't know grapes are a choking hazard?

An imposter mom, that's who.

THERE'S A PIVOTAL STORY IN GENESIS 3 where the serpent convinces Eve that if she eats fruit from the tree in the middle of the garden, she will be able to distinguish good and evil, just like God. She falls for the lie, takes a bite, and gives some to her husband, Adam. Suddenly, they both realize they're naked and feel shame for the very first time. When God walks through the garden later, looking for them, they hide.

God calls out a rhetorical question, "Where are you?"

I always picture Adam hanging his head as he confesses, "I heard the sound of you in the garden, and I was afraid, because I was naked, and I hid myself."

God responds again, with two more questions He already knows the answers to: "Who told you that you were naked? Have you eaten of the tree of which I commanded you not to eat?"[1]

Before this scene, God sees everything He's made—including Adam and Eve—and calls it "very good."[2] He gives the first humans on earth everything they need to live a whole, abundant life. Then the serpent comes along undermining God, questioning His character, and planting doubt, all under the guise of "Did God *actually* say that?"[3]

Eve listens to the serpent. Adam listens to Eve. Both of them listen to the wrong voice, sin enters the picture, and the world is never the same.

Let this be a lesson for us. Whenever we start hearing questionable narratives hissing, we need to ask ourselves, *Whose voice am I listening to?* Whenever we begin to hear things like *I'm an imposter, I'm a fraud, I'm a phony*—that's a good time to whip out the magnifying glass and reexamine the source.

Did God actually say this? Whose voice am I listening to?

I wish I could tell you at some point, imposter syndrome goes away. That you simply grow out of it, like a bad haircut. That once you've been a mom for twenty years, you no longer second-guess yourself. That once you get a book deal, you no longer feel like a fraud calling yourself a writer. If there is a unicorn woman out there who has mastered this level of confidence, I have yet to meet her. Meryl Streep herself once said in an interview, "Why would anyone want to see me again in a movie? And I don't know how to act anyway, so why am I doing this?"[4]

Meryl. Streep.

Dearest reader, hear me loud and clear: You are not an imposter mom. You have been called right here, right now, for such a time as this. God has placed you in this role, with these specific children, and you are exactly where you are supposed to be. *You are not a fraud.* Your

The enemy hisses *imposter* and *fraud,* but I beg you to listen to the louder voice who calls you by a different name.

writing, your music, your art, your gifts and talents and dreams—they have been planted in your heart intentionally, deliberately, masterfully on purpose by the Creator of the universe Himself. You have been appointed to steward all of it—these precious children under your care and this art burning a hole in your heart. There is no one better suited for this job, for this holy work, for this calling, than *you*.

The enemy hisses *imposter* and *fraud*, but I beg you to listen to the louder voice who calls you by a different name. The One who calls you Beloved. Free. Redeemed. Very good.

Write those words on your mirror. Write them in your heart.

And the next time you're tempted to believe you're a fraud, a phony, an imposter single-handedly running the biggest scam in the world pretending to be a real mom, a real artist, a real anything—I beg you to run to the nearest mirror, look yourself straight in the eyes, and ask: *Whose voice am I listening to?*

CREATIVE EXERCISE

Get an index card and write down a handful of names God calls you in Scripture. Make it colorful and pretty, like a personal art project. When you're done, tape the card to your bathroom mirror to serve as a reminder of what God says about you.

JOURNALING PROMPTS

Fold a piece of paper in half or draw a line down the center. On the left side, write out the most common lies that plague you as a mother and creative. On the right side, refute the lies with truth, by way of either written statements or Scripture.

6

ABUNDANCE OVER SCARCITY

"Fancy picnic awaits!" I yell into the abyss of our backyard, setting a tray of food down on a throw blanket in the middle of the patio. This is my modern-day version of ringing the dinner bell, only it's noon and instead of dinner I am serving a child-approved charcuterie tray: crackers, cheese, salami, strawberries, carrots, coconut sticks, and mini Larabars. It's a feast fit for three kids and then some.

Presley comes running first, plopping herself down on the blanket and digging in with a gleeful sigh. I retreat back inside the house to fix my own lunch, but before I even get to the kitchen, I hear the faint sound of hysterical crying outside. The sliding glass door opens and Carson yells into the house, "Mommy!! Presley isn't sharing the picnic!"

Rolling my eyes, I follow him outside to find my sweet two-year-old daughter hovering over the picnic tray like a mama bird guarding her nest, fresh tears running down her cheeks. I watch Everett reach around her hand to grab a cracker, and Presley screams, "HEY! DAT'S *MINE!*"

I stoop down to console her, and gently remind her the picnic is for everyone. "Honey, you need to share." She shakes her head no, her face crumpling again.

I point out the abundance of food, how the picnic contains more than enough items for her *and* her brothers. No matter how I phrase it, she refuses to believe me. A minute ago, she had been perfectly content sitting on the blanket eating alone. But the second another hand reached across the tray, she became threatened and possessive, as if her brothers had taken something directly from her, instead of their own portion.

She cries on and off for the remainder of lunchtime, shoveling strawberries into her mouth as if this is her last meal on earth, smearing her face with red juice and snot.

When all is said and done, once everyone's bellies are full and Presley is back to skipping around the trampoline without a care in the world, I can't help but notice there is still plenty of food left on the tray.

IN THE FIRST FEW YEARS of running Coffee + Crumbs, I noticed more motherhood websites popping up around the Internet like popcorn kernels exploding on the stove. *Pop! Pop! Pop!*

Many of these new sites appeared similar in style and structure, boasting "honest motherhood" as their tagline. *No need to panic,* I thought. *Surely there's enough room for all of us.* I slid my body down the metaphorical cafeteria bench, smiling and waving. *Hi, hello, nice to meet you, welcome to the lunch table.*

I studied their sites with curiosity and genuine interest, trying to figure out what each new motherhood platform was all about. Each space seemed rooted in a common goal to encourage mothers through stories. A good thing, no doubt. The more time I spent on each site, the more I believed Coffee + Crumbs still held its own as something sacred, something unique.

That is, until one day I realized some of these new sites had more Instagram followers than us, more Facebook likes than us, more comments on their blog posts than us. The initial growth and buzz Coffee + Crumbs experienced in the beginning had tapered off, and these new platforms were leaving us in the dust. They had ample resources to create innovative content I could only dream of making. Their staff seemed to surpass mine overnight. They had means to hire positions like a Business Operations Manager, a Senior Email Strategist, a Director of Finance and Accounting. In other words, they made so much money, they needed a *person* to *direct it*!

Hovered over my laptop late at night, I scoured for clues in the dark. *How are they growing so fast?! Where are they getting their money? How did they get all these Instagram followers? What's their secret?*

And the one question that plagued me most: *What am I doing wrong?*

Feelings of inadequacy arrived quickly, spreading over me like a whole-body rash. With fancy new motherhood platforms exploding to my left and right, I wondered if Coffee + Crumbs should keep going, or if we should throw in the towel while we could still quit with dignity. I had slid so far down the cafeteria bench, I teetered on the edge. If one more person sat down, I'd fall off.

Pop! Another new "storytelling community for moms" appeared in my Instagram feed.

My butt hit the floor. Even worse, no one seemed to notice. I looked up at all the sparkling new motherhood platforms, with their bajillion

Feelings of inadequacy arrived quickly, spreading over me like a whole-body rash.

followers and their shiny videos and graphics, eating and laughing on the bench without me.

(Pity, party of one? Your table is ready.)

Curled up in the fetal position on the floor, wallowing in a tidal wave of insecurity, I wondered, *Is there even still room for Coffee + Crumbs?*

AT THE ROOT, a scarcity mindset believes there is not enough to go around. This kind of thinking views everything in life as a pie—if one person takes a big piece, there's less for everyone else.

When we believe every hand reaching into the feast is taking some-thing away from us, we become stingy with everything we possess. We hoard our platforms. We stockpile our resources. We keep our hands positioned over the top of the picnic tray, guarding carefully what we deem to be ours. We keep intel to ourselves because we fear being ripped off. We create in a vacuum and we reject all offers to collaborate. We refuse to share our tools, our wealth, our spotlight, our everything.

My friend Adrienne once described notions of scarcity as "the enemy's signature on our thinking." When a scarcity mindset runs deep enough, we can become paralyzed from doing the good work God has called us to do. Furthermore, when we start to believe there's not enough room in the world for our talents and creative gifts, we can be tempted to stop creating altogether.

A few months ago, my friend Laura posted something to her Instagram feed the day before an almost identical post was scheduled to go up on my blog. There was a split second where I thought, *Oh no. This idea has already been taken. I can't publish this blog post anymore.* Honestly? There was even a fraction of a split second where I felt annoyed, borderline exasperated, as if Laura had done it on purpose, as if she had somehow snuck into my bedroom in the middle of the night and siphoned the idea straight out of my brain. THE NERVE OF THAT GIRL.

Obviously, that is crazy, and I came to my senses almost immediately. I ended up laughing and sending her a screenshot of my blog post with a shrugging emoji. *Guess God is putting the same message on our hearts this week!* She posted her words to Instagram. I posted mine to my blog. We both lived to tell about it, and we're still great friends.

The reality of creating art in a world filled with *other* people creating art is that, at some point, someone you know is going to create art similar to yours. This reality can be even harder to accept when someone you know climbs higher than you, faster than you, and beats you to the punch. One day you might be tinkering with a new podcast and *bam*—someone else will announce, *Hey guys, check out my new podcast!*

And it will have a cute name (a better name than yours), and their website will be pretty (much prettier than yours), and you'll think, *Oh well, I guess I shouldn't bother.*

When notions of scarcity creep into your mind, the enemy dances in delight.

He wants you to believe every idea has already been used. He wants to convince you the world already has enough poets, sculptors, florists, designers. He wants you to feel deeply threatened and unoriginal. He wants you to believe everyone else is already doing that thing you want to do. Not only that, he wants you to believe everyone else is doing that thing *better* than you ever could.

A scarcity mindset is more than just the enemy's signature on our thinking—it's one of the most powerful tools in his bag of tricks.

GROWING UP, my brother and I always received the exact same number of gifts on Christmas morning. I never really thought about this as a child, but now, as a mom of three, I get the strategy. Anytime I'm handing out something good, like cookies or candy, I make sure each kid gets the same amount. Within the walls of our home, this equal distribution keeps the stakes fair and the meltdowns at bay.

But what about out there? In the real world?

In the Gospel of Matthew, Jesus tells the story of a master who gives three servants different amounts of money: one servant receives five talents, one receives two talents, and one receives one talent. The servants who receive two and five talents go on to invest them wisely, turning around double what they've been given. The third servant, however, puts his one talent in the ground, rendering nothing extra.

The master is so pleased with the first two servants, he praises their faithfulness and promises to give them even more. Meanwhile, the

> God calls us to steward our portion, not compulsively keep track of everyone else's in a spreadsheet.

servant who sticks his single talent in the ground is chastised for his foolishness and then (double whammy!) is instructed to give his talent to the one who had the most.[1]

If there is jealousy or comparison brewing between the three servants, we don't see it acknowledged. If they're stewing in the corners of their bedrooms fighting about what is "fair," Jesus doesn't mention that.

The parable of the talents isn't about how much we receive, but rather *what we do* with *what we've been given.*

Every minute we spend resenting someone who possesses more talent, more accolades, more Instagram followers—is a minute we could be making something beautiful in a world hungry for hope. Every minute we spend wallowing in our own perceived lack, stirring up bitterness and animosity in our hearts, is a minute we could be living out our calling for the glory of our Maker.

We're not talking about a resource issue here.

We're talking about a *heart* issue.

When we consume ourselves with how much talent we have or don't have, what opportunities we get or don't get, this counting-slices-of-pie business becomes a significant distraction from our actual work. A scarcity mentality cultivates an ungrateful heart, and ultimately, questions the goodness, sufficiency, and generosity of our Father.

God calls us to steward our portion, not compulsively keep track of everyone else's in a spreadsheet.

EVERY DAY, I have to remind myself: God doles out the portions, and He knows the exact measure I am meant to have.

To some, my portion might look small and unimpressive. To others, my portion might look large. How my portion looks or appears is irrelevant, though, because my only responsibility is to take what God gives me—the specific, unique work with my name inscribed on it—and be a good steward of that gift.

If you've never seen the episode of *Friends* called "The One with All the Cheesecakes"—let me give you a quick recap. Chandler and Rachel eat a cheesecake delivered to their door by accident, and it turns out to be the best cheesecake they've ever tasted. The episode ends with a single slice of cheesecake falling to the floor in the hallway of their apartment complex, at which point they kneel down on the ground with forks, fighting over who gets the best crumbs.

The scene is comical, but sometimes I think that's what we look like when we allow a scarcity mindset to rule our lives.

Meanwhile, I can't help but wonder if God is thinking: *Do you not see this Willy Wonka factory I've created for you? There are aisles upon aisles of creative gifts and dreams and callings, all marked with your individual names, and you guys are still huddled on the floor, fighting over crumbs? Seriously?*

In His grace, God gently pulls us off the ground, away from the crumbs, away from the myth of scarcity. He redirects us and guides us toward something better: a heart posture that trusts in His goodness, His sufficiency, and His abundance. One that believes God will always give us what we need, and then some, to do whatever holy work He's called us to do.

The world declares all worthwhile things are in limited supply, on the way to running out. Meanwhile, God invites us to adopt a Kingdom mindset instead, one in which every thought we have and every decision we make is filtered through a lens of hope, love, and life beyond this earth. He invites us to share in His abundance, to be loyal stewards of every single gift He's placed in our hands. The best way we do that is by remembering who God is, what God cares about, and how God works.

I have been challenged and convicted in this arena a hundred times. One quick scroll of my prayer journals would reveal to you just how quickly I can fall back into a scarcity mindset. But here's a practice I've adopted that seems to be helping. Nowadays, whenever I see a new motherhood community pop up on the scene, I drop them an email. I introduce myself, introduce Coffee + Crumbs, and invite them to reach out if there's anything I can ever do to support their work.

When we believe in abundance, we give generously, even if we don't have a lot to give. When we believe there is enough for everyone, we are more inclined to share our resources, our money, our time, our praise, our knowledge, our platform, our everything. We are more inclined to celebrate those around us who are doing good work, to stand on the sidelines cheering till we're hoarse. We're quick to offer a helping hand, a resourceful tip. We're not stingy with our likes and shares and comments, but instead, we encourage others like crazy, inspiring those around us to do the same.

We stop fighting over crumbs, and finally get to enjoy the good stuff—the most extravagant picnic we've ever seen, masterfully designed by the God who loves every last one of us, who knows every single hair on our heads, who has thoughtfully and intentionally put out more than enough crackers and strawberries for all of His kids.

When we believe in abundance, we give generously, even if we don't have a lot to give.

CREATIVE EXERCISE

Make a sheet of homemade granola this week and divide it up into small jars to give away. Notice the sheer abundance of a single pan of granola, how many gifts can emerge from a single batch.

JOURNALING PROMPT

Have you ever been so busy fighting for crumbs you've lost sight of the portion of the feast meant for you? Write about it. How did God refine your heart in the midst of that struggle?

COCOA CHERRY GRANOLA

By Sarah Hauser

Yields 6–7 cups

3 cups	rolled oats
1 cup	roughly chopped almonds
¼ cup	cocoa powder
¼ teaspoon	kosher salt
½ cup	honey*
2 tablespoons	coconut oil, melted
1 teaspoon	vanilla extract
1 large	egg white
1½–2 cups	dried cherries

Preheat the oven to 300 degrees. Line a baking sheet with parchment paper and set aside.

In a large bowl, mix together the oats, almonds, cocoa powder, and salt. Then add the honey, coconut oil, and vanilla extract. Mix well.

In a separate small bowl, whisk the egg white until frothy. Stir the egg white into the granola mixture, and mix until fully incorporated.

Pour the granola out onto the prepared baking sheet. Use a spoon (or your hands) to spread it out into an even layer. Gently press down on the granola to help it stick together.

Bake for about 40–50 minutes, rotating the pan halfway through to ensure even cooking. The granola should darken slightly and feel mostly dry to the touch. (If you're using a dark baking sheet, you may need to decrease the baking time. In that case, check the granola after 35–38 minutes.)

Remove from the oven and let the granola cool completely (resist the urge to stir!). It will get more crisp and crunchy as it cools. When it's cool, break up the granola into whatever size clusters you like, and stir in the dried cherries.

The granola will keep in an airtight container at room temperature for a couple weeks. For a longer shelf life, store it in the freezer.

The recipe as written makes a slightly sweetened cocoa granola—the sweetness level of a very dark chocolate. Feel free to add more honey if you want the finished product to be sweeter.

7

BREADCRUMBS AND LADYBUGS

I've always loved the description of pursuing a calling as "following the breadcrumbs." Like a character in a fairy tale, I picture myself zigzagging through a forest following the breadcrumbs God drops in front of me as a path begins to form. A crumb here, a crumb there. *What's next, God? What do you have in store for me today?*

A breadcrumb can be anything: an opened door, an answered prayer, a fully formed idea flying into my head in the shower. It could be an introduction to the right person at the perfect time, or a kind email from a stranger arriving on a day I am feeling discouraged. It could be a passage of Scripture meeting me right where I am, or puzzle pieces of a problem suddenly clicking into place with ease.

Breadcrumbs are made of peace and lined with grace. When you stumble across one, there is no mistaking where it came from. These divine hints lead us forward, as if God Himself is holding out His hand, pulling us along to the next chapter He is writing in our lives. We cannot conjure breadcrumbs up. We cannot predict which direction they will lead, how many we will find, or when they will appear. But they always arrive right on time, in the perfect proportion, like manna.

There is both a mystery and a certainty to the act of following breadcrumbs.

I believe this is what it means to have faith.

IN THE SECOND HALF OF 2019, I became unexpectedly restless in my creative work. I battled a toxic combination of stress and disinterest, anxiety and apathy. I started to doubt every single thing I was doing, from writing to managing Coffee + Crumbs, to having public social media accounts. I felt burnt out, zapped of creative energy, and, perhaps the most distressing, completely void of passion.

On one particular creative dark night of the soul, I started drafting The Letter in my head, the one where I would announce the end of Coffee + Crumbs. I thought about how I'd tell the writers, how I'd tell my friends and family. I thought through the logistics: how long I'd pay to keep the archives up, how I'd gradually shut all the pieces down, what goodbye gifts I'd purchase for the team.

I prayed for clarity, waiting for an answer. For weeks, I kept my unsettling 3:00 a.m. thoughts to myself, not wanting to alarm my husband or coworkers until I was sure. On good days, I trudged along with a hollow heart, checking items off my to-do list like a well-programmed robot. On bad days, I began to mentally accept that

Breadcrumbs are made of peace and lined with grace. When you stumble across one, there is no mistaking where it came from.

everything I'd invested my creative energy into over the past five years had finally come to an end.

The well had run dry, once and for all.

Weary, depleted, and on the verge of quitting everything—I started seeing ladybugs everywhere.

I SEE THE FIRST ONE IN THE KITCHEN. She creeps along the counter, minding her own business, weaving in and out of lingering breakfast remnants. After watching her for a minute, eventually I snap out of my trance and carry her to the camellia tree outside our front door, carefully placing her on a leaf.

I am not the type to pick up a bug and take it outside. I regularly smash spiders with magazines, vacuum up ants, swat flies with a towel. On the rare occasion a particularly large insect invades our home, I recruit my husband. I remember one day, early in our marriage, I was home alone when I saw a gigantic black spider run across the tile floor. I grabbed a thick magazine and tossed it like a horseshoe—*splat*—crushing, I assumed, the spider in an instant. Too terrified to confirm its death, I dropped three books on top of the magazine and left it for Brett to deal with later.

(I'm not some kind of bug savior, is what I'm trying to say.)

I find the second one in the bathroom. I am applying mascara when something flutters behind me, catching my eye. I turn around to find another ladybug, crawling up the window.

Before you start wondering if my house is infested with ladybugs, let me tell you about the third: I am sitting at a red light one day when a ladybug lands on my windshield. Literally, right in my line of sight, waiting at an intersection, on an ordinary Tuesday morning.

"I know this sounds crazy," I tell my husband that night, "but I'm seeing ladybugs everywhere and I feel like God is trying to tell me something."

A few weeks later, my friend Sonya and I are talking about writing and faith, and, I think, tattoos? I can't remember how the conversation begins, but at some point our discussion turns to feathers. She tells me that along her creative journey, God has used feathers to nudge her to keep going, and that whenever she starts to question or doubt whether writing is something she should pursue, a feather appears.

This quickly becomes a thing between us: I start texting Sonya pictures of all the ladybugs I encounter, and she texts me back pictures of feathers. Like two breadcrumbs, there they are—a sign for her, a sign for me. A ladybug on a windowsill. A feather on a sidewalk. *Let's keep going. Don't give up. I won't if you won't.*

I begin standing still, listening, paying attention. Not just to the ladybugs, but to everything around me: my surroundings, my thoughts, things people say to me, anything and everything God could be leading me toward. Slowly, gradually, something in my heart starts to shift, a surrendering of sorts. I begin noticing beauty again, everywhere, just like I used to. I start to feel an inkling of creative energy stirring, a faint pulse reviving.

One day, I wake up and actually feel a desire to create again, to get words down on paper.

Another ladybug appears on the living room curtain. I start dreaming of a new narrative podcast, a website makeover, a workshop I'd like to teach someday. The fifth ladybug shows up in my kitchen sink, the sixth on the bathroom counter. *Be still. Listen. Pay attention.*

I toy with the idea of starting a newsletter. My head buzzes with possibilities, and dare I say, a glimmer of confidence. For the first time in months, I do not feel paralyzed or creatively dead inside.

Let me tell you about the seventh.

I am standing in the shower washing my hair when I get hit with a mental lightning bolt. A flurry of ideas appears, one after the other, like a pitching machine hurling balls at my head. I feel dizzy and disoriented, thrilled and confused. But mostly, terrified of losing the inspiration.

I hop out of the shower, throw on a bathrobe, twist my hair up in a towel, and grab a notebook. Scribbling furiously, I fill up four pages over the next thirty minutes with stories and anecdotes and metaphors, all connected to the parallels between motherhood and creativity. On top of the frenzy and elation, I also experience a weird sense of déjà vu—me, six years ago, standing in a different shower in a different

> I begin standing still, listening, paying attention. Not just to the ladybugs, but to everything around me.

house, being hit with the idea for Coffee + Crumbs, a concept so fully formed, I knew it couldn't possibly have come from me.

When I confide in a friend about the experience later, she responds, "Isn't it incredible when we get to co-create with God like that?"

Two nights after I scribble the shower ideas down in a notepad (it would turn out to be the first outline for the book you're holding in your hands), on my way to the kitchen to get a glass of water, I notice a speck on my bedspread out of the corner of my eye.

It is, of course, a ladybug.

LADYBUGS CONTINUE TO SHOW UP IN MY PATH, literally and figuratively.

In the weeks leading up to my book proposal deadline, I booked myself a night at a hotel to finish my proposal. The morning before I left town, I woke up a little before 6:00 a.m. and worked through my

JENA HOLLIDAY

ARTIST, ILLUSTRATOR, AUTHOR, STORYTELLER
@ASPOONFULOFFAITH
MINNEAPOLIS, MINNESOTA

Q: How does your faith inspire or affect your creative work?
A: My faith is a large part of the reason I even began to share my creativity and my creative work. It's the heartbeat of why I continue to show up. In seasons when I felt like what I made didn't matter—God was right there reminding me we were doing this together. In small moments, through conversations with friends and even strangers, I was told something I created or shared spoke to them, encouraged them, helped them hold on. That's how I am inspired: I know this is all much bigger than me.

usual quiet time routine: read, pray, write. I had been fighting feelings of insecurity all week, and that morning, in a moment of doubt, I prayed for a ladybug.

A few hours later, I got in the car to make the forty-five-minute drive to the hotel. Sitting in my driveway, I opened up my Voxer app and saw a text message from a new friend. We had recently taken a writing workshop together, and she was one of only a handful of people who even knew I was working on a book.

That morning she reached out to specifically encourage me in my writing. Her text ended with: "I need your book and so do so many others."

The time stamp on her message? 6:23 a.m. Within five minutes, give or take, of my asking God for a ladybug.

There's a story in the Gospel of John where Jesus heals an official's son simply by saying, "Go, your son will live." On the way home, his

servants meet him halfway to share the good news: his son was already getting better! The official asks his servants what time the fever left his son, and they tell him in the seventh hour. The official immediately connects the dots—his son had been healed the same hour Jesus spoke.[1]

When I saw the time stamp on my friend's message, I knew the timing carried significance. Because what are the odds? What are the odds one of the few people who even knew about this book would feel prompted to encourage me at *the exact same time* I asked God for a ladybug?

The world would call this a coincidence, but I don't believe in coincidences. I believe in God. And I believe He is working, all of the time, connecting us to Himself and to each other. He's laying out breadcrumbs. Directing the flight paths of ladybugs. He's orchestrating where the feathers fall.

When publishers began expressing interest in this book, my imposter syndrome skyrocketed. In the midst of meeting with acquisition editors and Very Important Publishing People, I asked God for another ladybug the week of my birthday.

I felt pathetic asking again, ashamed of my lack of faith. *What is wrong with me? Why do I keep doubting that God wants me to write this book?*

I was so desperate for a sign, I didn't just pray for a ladybug, I prayed for a ladybug *in the house*. Even now, I don't know what possessed me to ask God for something so wildly specific, but I did. I had been seeing ladybugs for over a year, and at the height of that

The world would call this a coincidence, but I don't believe in coincidences.

make-or-break moment with publishers, I wanted nothing more than a full circle moment. *Me. God. Book. Ladybug.*

The day after my birthday, Everett ran into my bedroom.

"Mommy! There's a ladybug on the kitchen window!!!"

I started running toward the kitchen, almost in disbelief that I'd actually find what I had asked God for, again. But sure enough, I did. There it was, a ladybug crawling up the window. Not on the outside of the glass. On the *inside* of the glass.

I started to cry.

Not just for the ladybug, but for all of it. For the way God met me in a dark, empty creative season and turned the light on for me. For the way He didn't let me walk away from a job I loved just because I had grown weary and uninspired doing it. For the way He gently picked me up out of my comfort zone and dropped me down someplace new, where everything grey turned into color again. For the way He swooped in and refilled my empty well.

For the way He reminded me I am never creating alone.

YEARS BEFORE THE LADYBUGS, two of my biggest breadcrumbs arrived in the form of other people's prayers.

When I was pregnant with my first baby, my friend Camille prayed over me one night at a Bible study. It was one of those prayers that feels like a small earthquake. She boldly proclaimed motherhood would be a "broad calling for me"—that other women would feel drawn to me for mentoring and encouragement.

At the time, I had no idea what her words meant. But a year and a half later, God gave me the idea for Coffee + Crumbs.

Lauren Winner writes in *Girl Meets God*: "God is a novelist. He uses all sorts of literary devices: alliteration, assonance, rhyme, synecdoche, onomatopoeia. But of all of these, His favorite is foreshadowing."[2]

Many years later, at a speaking engagement, a complete stranger asked if she could pray over me at the end of the event. With her hands firmly planted on my shoulders, she said: "God is going to provide supernatural ways for things to come together with ease—books, projects, and all the things He has in store for you."

Again, at the time, I had no idea what those words meant. But a little over a year later, I'd go on to sign with a dream literary agent, somehow complete a book proposal during a global pandemic, and have multiple publishers interested in my words—all while seeing ladybugs everywhere.

Supernatural ways.

Things will come together.

All the things He has in store for you.

WHEN I BECAME A MOTHER, my senses seemed to intensify overnight. It's how I can smell a dirty diaper a mile away, just like I can hear a child reaching into the snack drawer from the other side of the house. At times, I've found this constant alertness to be . . . *exhausting.* Even if I wanted to, I can't seem to shut off my heightened senses— they reflect one way motherhood has profoundly changed me.

Over time, though, I've come to appreciate the parallel between staying alert as a mother and staying alert as a creative. Both motherhood and creativity require us to pay attention, to listen, to remain expectant.

I don't know the state of your creative spirit today. You may be feeling depleted, jaded, uninspired, or confused. You may be striving, hoping, or waiting for clarity that never seems to come. You may be lost, anxious, frustrated, or unsure where to turn next. Maybe you're on the verge of giving up. Maybe you're on the verge of quitting everything.

Before you do, will you try something?

Ask God for a breadcrumb.

Commit a period of time to rest, prayer, and quiet. Ask God for guidance, for discernment, for eyes to see and ears to hear. Be still. Listen. Pay attention to what you notice in Scripture, in conversations, in nature. Stay expectant. Keep track of the serendipitous text messages, the creatures or landscapes or things you keep encountering, repeated messages and themes. What do you keep seeing, over and over again? What do you keep hearing? Where do you sense the Holy Spirit stirring in you?

Write it all down. Even if you don't understand the message at the time. Even if what you're hearing makes no sense. Because one day, a year from now, or maybe five, maybe more, you'll be able to see the

FUN FACT

When most people think of ladybug wings, they picture a red base with black polka dots. But the hind wings—the *alae*—are what actually allow a ladybug to fly. These wings are four times the size of a ladybug itself and can move in every direction: up, down, forward, backward. They are powerful enough to keep a ladybug in the air for up to two hours, reaching speeds up to thirty-seven miles per hour and altitudes as high as three Empire State Buildings stacked on top of each other.

When not in use, these wings fold up neatly inside a protective shell.

Like a Pack 'n Play perfectly folding down to fit inside a bag, ladybugs fold their alae into a sleek package, tucking them into a slender sliver of space between their abdomen and outer wings.[3]

I believe this is a beautiful metaphor for the creative process. While the world may recognize us by our "outer wings"—the visible, shiny accomplishments—we would never be able to fly at all without a source of inner strength. For it is the Spirit of God, tucked perfectly in our souls, who is guiding us to new forms of inspiration, leading us to the next breadcrumb, carrying us home.

trail of breadcrumbs behind you. How every sign, every message, every ladybug has led you to where you are.

Someday you'll be able to see the mystery and the certainty of it all, as you continue learning how to create by faith.

CREATIVE EXERCISE

Take a walk in complete silence. No headphones, no music, no podcast. Just walk, listen, and keep your heart tuned to anything God might want to share with you.

JOURNALING PROMPT

What are the "breadcrumbs" or "ladybugs" in your own life? Write about an instance where you have significantly experienced God's hand in your creative journey. If nothing comes to mind, that's okay. Consider writing a prayer instead, perhaps asking God for guidance and direction in any area you feel lost.

8

RADICAL OBEDIENCE

Roughly five months before my manuscript is due, my parents generously offer to take me and my family on a week-long vacation.

Before the trip, I pop into Kinkos to print a copy of my book-in-progress. This feels like A Very Big Deal, exporting close to 25,000 words. I run my fingers over the freshly printed stack of paper, clip all forty-eight pages to a clipboard, and slip it in the front zipper pocket of my suitcase with a red pen.

Between acclimating to the time change, the hustle and bustle of daily activities, and the (delightful) exhaustion that accompanies traveling with three young children, I do not even pull the manuscript out of my suitcase until our second to last night.

And here's where I wish I could tell you something magical happened. Here's where I wish I could tell you I sat underneath the palm trees, ocean air caressing my face, inspiration striking just as a ladybug serendipitously landed on my knee. Here's where I wish I could tell you I brilliantly marked up every page with my red pen, slicing and dicing until the words glimmered like the magnificent sunset in front of me.

(We all know where this is going, right?)

In reality, I take my clipboard manuscript down to a chair around the corner from the pool. Right away I notice the air is full of smoke. There is a fire raging nearby, causing neighboring residents to be evacuated. By the time I settle into my chair, the wind is picking up and employees begin passing out flyers encouraging people to stay in their rooms.

Thirty minutes, I tell myself. *I'm just going to stay down here and work on my book for thirty minutes.*

The papers begin whipping up and down in the wind, eager to escape the clipboard, while my own hair starts slapping me in the face. Conditions are less than ideal, but I am determined to make *some* kind of progress on this manuscript tonight, even if it means doing so in between a fire and a hurricane.

I begin reading my introduction. And right away, I feel sick. Not sick like I've eaten bad chicken, and not sick like I'm on a boat, but the type of sick you feel when you realize this big, important, significant thing you've been working on for the better part of a year is . . . *not good.*

My heart beats faster. My inner monologue starts to spiral. *This sentence is garbage. That metaphor is such a cliche. Oh my gosh, this book is terrible. Awful. How did this happen?! How did I not see it? Maybe it'll get better. Maybe it'll get better. Maybe it'll get better.*

(Narrator: it does not get better.)

I take my red pen and start slashing, writing comments in the margins, scribbling incoherent thoughts.

The wind is turning vicious, howling in my ears. Suddenly I have ink all over me—on my fingers, my wrist, my elbow. I look down and my pen is dripping, leaking inexplicably. I shake it off and keep going, keep correcting, keep revising, keep trying to fix what sounded so beautiful in my head, but is so broken on this fourteen-cent Kinkos page.

A speck of dust flies into my eye, irritating my contact lens. My drink tips over with the next gust of wind, spraying frothy pineapple juice on my dress. My eyes burn with tears. I'm not sure if the dust is to blame, or if I'm simply grieving my own lack of talent. I blink a few times, trying to focus my eyes, but all I see is more ink, more red, all over my fingers.

I want to scream.

I chuck the pen in the trash and go to the bathroom to wash my hands. Then I return for round two, because I am a glutton for punishment. New pen. Back to the chair. More smoke. More wind. Everyone else is heading back to their rooms.

Not me.

I sit down and force myself to keep reading. My lungs feel constricted. My palms begin to sweat. My heart is practically beating out of my chest. *This is the worst thing I've written in my entire life. I have to fix it. I have to start over. Wait. I don't have time to start over.* I want to throw up. I want to cry. I want to jump in the pool with the clipboard and watch the ink smear into the water, a much-needed baptism.

I look up at the palm trees swaying over my head so violently they look like they could snap, and I raise the white flag, only eight pages in.

I head back to my room a walking tragedy, my skin stained with ink, my dress splattered with juice, my eyes filled with tears.

ONE MIGHT ASSUME A BLANK PAGE is a writer's best friend—a clean canvas, ripe with opportunity, just waiting to meet its full potential. But for me, a blank page often represents one thing and one thing only: impending failure.

I want to write something perfect, but I know I cannot write something perfect, so I sit, frozen, queasy, with panicky fingers hovering over the laptop keys, paralyzed by my own impossibly high standards.

Sometimes I give up before I even start. Do you know how many stories I haven't written simply because I knew, deep in my bones, I wouldn't be able to write them perfectly?

If and when I manage to push past the initial performance anxiety, my perfectionism quickly morphs into phase two—attacking my work the second it comes out of my brain. I type, then delete. Type. Delete. Everything I type, I immediately delete. Nobody picks apart

Nobody picks apart my creative work as harshly as I do. I'm like my own personal Internet troll.

my creative work as harshly as I do. I'm like my own personal Internet troll. *This is garbage. This is garbage. This is garbage.*

My friend Hannah Brencher calls this form of aggressive self-editing "bringing a chainsaw into the writing room."[1] And she forbids it. *But, Hannah,* I want to tell her, *I love my chainsaw collection.* I have one for unimpressive words, one for poorly written sentences, and one for dumb ideas. I am a chainsaw connoisseur!

Just yesterday I took one of my chainsaws to an entire page approximately thirty seconds after I finished writing it. Poof, gone, like a dead tree. *Good riddance.* I tossed the remnants into the wood chipper until they turned into dust and flew away with the wind.

"Be willing to be a bad artist," Julia Cameron coaxes in *The Artist's Way*.[2] She says if someone is willing to be a bad artist, they "have a chance to be an artist, and, perhaps, over time, a very good one."

Sorry, Julia. You lost me at "bad." I prefer perfect or nothing.

This is one of my greatest stumbling blocks: Writing badly is the gateway to writing at all, but I want to write perfectly on the first try. I'd rather sit in a chair for three hours deleting every single word I write than compose a terrible first draft and be forced to face my own lack of talent on the page.

A FEW MONTHS INTO DISTANCE LEARNING during the COVID pandemic, I am genuinely surprised at how well Carson's kindergarten teacher is corralling a bunch of five-year-olds through pixels. They begin and end every day with music, the lyrics of which I now know by heart. I can count on the teacher's sing-song voice to carry through the house via Zoom at 9:00 a.m. and 11:45 a.m., Monday through Friday.

All of their assignments—a mix of phonics, math, reading, and writing—are given through videos in an app called Seesaw. Carson conducts school in the living room, which means I inevitably hear snippets of the videos as I shuffle around the house.

"And remember," Miss Julie says at the end of every video, pausing for emphasis, "*always try your best*—it doesn't *ever* have to be perfect."

After I hear those words more than a hundred times, eventually they get stuck in my head. Pretty soon I start repeating them to myself whenever I sit down to write. *Remember, just try your best. It doesn't ever have to be perfect.*

I've always considered the opposite of perfect to be "good enough"—a far lower standard appropriate for plenty of occasions. For example, when I'm too tired to deep clean my house, I simply tidy up the toys and run a quick vacuum across the floors. *Good enough.* Sometimes (most of the time?) I only shave the bottom half of my legs. I never fold underwear or pajamas; I just throw them in the drawer. Don't tell my dentist, but I only floss after I eat popcorn. *Good enough, good enough, good enough.*

When it comes to my art, though, I don't *want* to create "good enough" work. I don't want to settle for the minimum effort. And

ELSIE GOODWIN

FIBER ARTIST
@REFORMFIBERS
CLAREMONT, CALIFORNIA

Q: If you could give moms who long to create as they raise their children a word of advice or encouragement, what would it be?
A: The process of creating is what is truly fulfilling—not the money, or the validation, or anything else. When I first started creating, I began with super small projects. I would challenge myself to learn something new: work with new yarn, learn a new stitch, mess up, try again, mess up, try again. First crochet, then knitting, then macramé, a little punch needle, embroidery, sewing, weaving, etc. A lot of my work is still bad, a lot of it is given away to loved ones as gifts, but through it all I know I am the one giving the gift to myself . . . the time to create.

yet, I know perfect is an impossible standard. So where does that leave me?

I'm looking for something in the middle—something in between perfect and good enough. If perfect is too high a standard, and good enough is too low a standard, what's a happy medium?

What do we call the act of *actually* trying our best?

IN MARK 14, Jesus is reclining at a table in Simon's house when a woman walks in carrying an alabaster flask of pure nard, an expensive scented oil. The bottle of perfume is worth over three hundred denarii, equivalent to a year's salary.

The woman breaks the jar and pours perfume on Jesus' head, anointing him, while everyone else in the room looks on in horror. Some start scolding her immediately for wasting such an extravagant commodity. They point out that the woman could have sold the jar for heaps of money and given the proceeds to the poor.

Jesus, though, offers a different response. He says, "Leave her alone. Why do you trouble her? She has done a beautiful thing to me."[3]

The woman gives Jesus her most expensive possession, her most valuable offering, the best of what she had.

Jesus goes on to say, "She has done what she could; she has anointed my body beforehand for burial. And truly, I say to you, wherever the gospel is proclaimed in the whole world, what she has done will be told in memory of her."[4]

While others in the room are quick to accuse, ridicule, and criticize the woman for wasting such an indulgent offering, Jesus boldly presents a different narrative. *She has done a beautiful thing. She has done what she could.*

In his book *Secrets of the Secret Place*, Bob Sorge writes: "Radical obedience does not seek to comply to the minimal standards but pursues extravagant, lavish fulfillment."[5]

Like the woman with the perfume, giving Jesus the *best* of what we have—the best of our time, our effort, our talent—is never a waste. Extravagant, lavish fulfillment is never lost on Him.

Could radical obedience be the middle place between perfection and good enough? Or perhaps not even a middle place, but a better way altogether?

Radical obedience does not pursue perfection but aims to please the One who is perfect. Radical obedience does not settle for good enough, but aims to fulfill Colossians 3:23—"Whatever you do, work at it with all your heart."[6]

My boys do not always have a cheerful attitude when I ask them to clean their room. Sometimes I hear them grumbling under their breath, or I can just tell by the way they softly stomp away. Those same darling children occasionally take shortcuts by picking everything up off the carpet, toys and socks and books, and shoving the whole collection under their bunk beds, or into a random drawer.

Could radical obedience be the middle place between perfection and good enough? Or perhaps not even a middle place, but a better way altogether?

As a mom, I am irritated by this behavior.

As an artist, I stand convicted.

How many times have I huffed and puffed when God has nudged me to write something I didn't feel like writing? Or called me to speak on a stage I didn't want to get up on? How many times have I considered running the opposite direction of where God has called me? How many times have I cut corners?

Radical obedience, at the heart, is the sheer act of saying, "Yes, Lord." *Yes, I'll go there. Yes, I'll do that. I'll give you my best effort because YOU are worthy of my best offering.* Radical obedience is a zealous commitment to fulfilling whatever holy work God sets in front of our hands.

This means where God calls, we go. When God calls us to write, we write. When God asks us to sing, we sing. As artists made in the image of the ultimate Artist, we paint and draw and sew and sculpt, not bitterly or lazily, but with enthusiasm, devotion, and a sense of joyful eagerness to participate. Because when we link arms with our Creator to do what He uniquely designed us to do, we usher a bit of the Kingdom into this world—and God gets the glory for it.

On the outside, radical obedience and perfectionism look similar: a commitment to pursuing our work with excellence. On the inside, though, the motivations are wildly different. Perfectionism seeks to please man, but radical obedience seeks to please God.

Perfectionism is rooted in anxiety, frustration, and endless striving. Radical obedience is rooted in peace, joy, and endless surrender. Perfectionism chokes, paralyzes, and prevents us from even starting. Radical obedience launches, spurs, and propels us forward.

For most of my life, I've tried to make everything I create as lovely and flawless as possible. I'm learning this level of dedication can be a strength or a weakness, depending on the heart posture hiding underneath.

Am I seeking my own glory?

Or am I seeking lavish, extravagant fulfillment of what God's asked of me?

I AM STANDING IN THE KITCHEN emptying the dishwasher when I hear a gut-wrenching howl echo across the house.

Presley is independently working on a fine motor activity in her bedroom. Little wooden boards are scattered around the carpet with pictures on them—a butterfly, a train, a snail. The pictures are made up of colorful shapes, and Presley is attempting to put matching tiles on top of each board to build the pictures.

I hear another growl. Another primal scream. I pause emptying the dishwasher, debating whether or not I should go check on her. Before I have the chance to decide, she comes stomping down the hall, screaming, "I CAN'T! DO! *ANYFING*!!!"

Perfectionism is rooted in anxiety, frustration, and endless striving. Radical obedience is rooted in peace, joy, and endless surrender.

She appears at the doorway of the kitchen, exasperated, tears streaming down her face, brows furrowed. I take her into my arms, and she lets out one more thunderous howl for dramatic effect. I wipe the tears from her face, tell her everything is going to be okay, and offer to accompany her back to the bedroom.

I lie down on the carpet and watch her try again. She knows how to pick up the tiles and put them where they need to be, but her chubby fingers keep bumping the other pieces in the process, causing the whole picture to get messed up. With every accidental bump, every mistake, she lets out an emphatic *UGGGGHHHHHH!*

More tears, more frustration.

"Pres, take a deep breath," I tell her in a soft voice. "It's okay. Look at Momma. See how I breathe? In, and out."

I model: inhale, exhale. Inhale, exhale. She copies me, blowing out her exhales with a dramatic *whooooosh* sound.

"Hey!" she says, surprised, "I do fewl bedder!"

For the next several minutes, she huffs and puffs through her concentration, breathing as if she's in a Lamaze class. At one point, her hand accidentally knocks half the tiles off the butterfly board and she pounds her fist on the carpet with a frustrated groan.

I simply lie there next to her, bearing witness to her struggle, one I know by heart. I know what it feels like to want to throw a puzzle across the room, because I know what it feels like to want to chuck an entire manuscript in the pool.

She takes another deep breath, collecting herself, and looks at me. I see a hint of relief in her eyes, as if she suddenly remembers I am there. As if she forgot, for a minute, that she wasn't alone.

"Momma, can you help me?" she asks, swiping a piece of hair out of her face.

I smile, honored to be asked. "I'd love to help you," I tell her.

We spend the next twenty minutes on the floor, her laying down shapes, me course correcting when they bump out of alignment, until every board is complete.

That's all we can do, isn't it? As mothers. As artists. We do the work. We ask for help. We show up and give God our best effort, our richest offering, hoping someday we meet our Maker and hear "She has done a beautiful thing. She has done what she could."

CREATIVE EXERCISE

Do something this week you *know* you cannot do perfectly. Take note of how you feel. Do you feel a sense of frustration? Or freedom?

JOURNALING PROMPT

Write about a time you've struggled with perfectionism. Then, write about a time you've practiced radical obedience. Compare and contrast the two stories. What do you notice?

9

THE ARK DIDN'T
BUILD ITSELF

After our boys ask no less than a dozen times, my husband and I finally give in: "Yes, you can do a lemonade stand."

Already plotting what they will purchase with their profits (see: LEGOs), Everett and Carson are gleaming in the back seat as we venture to Target for supplies. In the juice and soda aisle, I offer to fund their start-up expenses.

"Remember, you'll have to pay me back for the cost of supplies when the lemonade stand closes," I tell them.

They nod in agreement, carefully selecting cups, poster boards, plastic pitchers, lemonade powder, and—to give them a competitive edge over *other* stands in the neighborhood—Popsicles. Everett keeps a running tally of the cost, and I silently congratulate myself on the math lesson I've just unintentionally orchestrated.

At home, I conduct market research in a local moms Facebook group to assess the going rate for lemonade, while the boys spread out all over the dining room floor with their posters and art supplies. We land on fifty cents for lemonade and one dollar for Popsicles, filling their toy cash register with dollar bills and quarters to create change. In the kitchen, the boys drop scoops of lemonade powder into two pitchers, one regular and one pink, *oooohing* and *aaaahing* as the powder dissolves in the water like a science experiment.

Finally, we drag their little wooden homework desks out to the bottom of the driveway to set up shop. Everett and Carson ride their scooters down to the end of the street and tape a poster to the stop sign with an arrow pointing toward our house. They hold the other signs in their hands and start jumping up and down yelling, "Lemonaaaaaade!!!"

It takes twenty minutes for the first customer to arrive, but business picks up shortly after. Most of the neighbors trickle by, and a number of cars stop at the curb, handing dollar bills out the window as if cruising through a drive-thru. Throughout the day, Brett and I remind the boys about the importance of good customer service. *Don't assume the change is a tip. Grab Popsicles from the bottom of the cooler, not the top. Make sure you wipe up the spills. Don't forget to say, "Thank you, have a great day!"*

Sweat drips down the sides of their faces all afternoon. At the end of the day, even after paying me back for the supplies, they earn close to fifty dollars. We set aside money for tithing and saving, and we agree they can use the rest to buy a small LEGO set.

Later that night, relaying the day's events, I ask the boys if they had fun, and if they'd ever want to do a lemonade stand again.

Everett looks at me with a solemn face and nods. "Yeah, but it was a *lot* of work."

I stifle a laugh and smile at him the way a parent does when they realize their child has learned a valuable life lesson.

AFTER I HAD BEEN BLOGGING FOR A FEW YEARS, someone emailed me and asked for writing advice. I don't remember every facet of my response, but I do remember offering her what was, at the time, my go-to formula: *Just write when you're inspired.*

I said this, of course, with the confidence (naïveté?) of a young twenty-something who possessed all the spare time in the world. Back then, I believed writers should only write if they were "in the mood."

Over a decade and three kids later, if you asked me for writing advice today, this is what I'd tell you: Write when you're inspired, absolutely . . . but also write when you're not.

If you can drop what you're doing the second lightning bolts of inspiration hit your brain, by all means, GO. We all know how quickly an idea can enter and exit the mind. Sometimes it's gone in a flash, like a train zipping through a tunnel. If we don't catch an idea the second it sparks, grab on for dear life, and wrestle it down onto paper or into the notes section of our phone, the entire thought can disappear into thin air like a puff of smoke. There's a reason I keep a notepad within four steps of the shower.

But if we sit around simply *waiting* for inspiration to strike, one of two things will happen:

1) We will go weeks without creating anything at all.
2) When inspiration finally does strike, one of our kids will have to poop.

A decade ago, I did not practice regular discipline in my creativity because, simply put, I did not have to. Even with a full-time job, I had extra hours in my week. I had the margin and white space and bandwidth to create whenever inspiration struck.

My motto then: put your butt in the chair when you feel like it.

My motto today: put your butt in the chair even when you don't.

In *Bittersweet*, Shauna Niequist writes about letting her son choose how he sits at the dinner table. He has to sit, no matter what, but he can choose knees or buns. She writes,

> Creativity isn't easy, and it isn't something you turn on like a light switch. My inbox will tell you that the world is full of writers who don't write, painters who don't paint, dancers who don't dance. They want me to tell them something, ostensibly a secret something that will get them up and moving again, creating again. My reply is always a disappointing one: I don't know what to tell you. Sit down, knees or buns.[1]

What a frustrating truth, to learn there is no such thing as a magic trick, no such thing as a secret sauce. We can talk all day about wanting to write, wanting to make a podcast, wanting to garden, but *wanting* to create is not enough. You have to *want* to do it, and, well, then you have to *actually do it*.

I won't lie to you: this part is difficult.

Often when it's time to put my butt in the chair, I get a sudden urge to do anything else. Text a friend. Check my email. Rearrange the furniture. Look at homes on Zillow I will never be able to afford. Go on Pinterest to pin recipes I will never make, surf Target.com to look at shoes I may or may not buy. Start a load of laundry, water the plants, and end up eating a plate of leftover pasta, staring out the window.

Sometimes the simple act of showing up—body, mind, and soul—is the hardest part of the creative process.

What a frustrating truth, to learn there is no such thing as a magic trick, no such thing as a secret sauce.

And here's where I have to give a little bit of tough love: *this part is on us.*

Nobody is going to force us to get up at 5:00 a.m. (maybe a crying baby, but they don't care if we create or not). Nobody is going to walk into our homes and shut off Netflix on our behalf. Nobody is going to gently grab the phone out of our hands and tell us to stop scrolling Instagram.

This part of the creative process is kind of like giving birth. We can be surrounded by midwives and doulas and nurses, our husbands, our moms, whoever, and they can all be helping us, coaching us, holding our legs back and wiping sweaty strands of hair off our foreheads. Ultimately, though, *we* are the ones who have to show up in that moment.

Because we are the only ones who can push.

HAVE YOU EVER WONDERED if Noah didn't feel like showing up to work on the ark?

Talk about an undertaking. Building a three-story boat, plank by plank, before power tools were invented? To quote Everett and his lemonade stand, it sounds like *a lot of work.* I wonder if Noah showed up every day with a positive, can-do attitude, or if occasionally he woke up and sighed, "Really, Lord? This, again?"

We know, more than anything, that building the ark required a tremendous amount of faith. But building the ark also required discipline—the steady commitment to showing up, day after day, sweating in the sun, pounding away on wood for hours on end until the job was complete.

In the end, Noah's labor resulted in far more than a simple ark that stayed afloat. All those hours co-laboring with God led to something far greater: a rainbow, a promise, a covenant between God and every living creature on earth.

ELISE CRIPE

CRAFTER, MAKER OF EVERYTHING
@ELISEJOY
EL DORADO HILLS, CALIFORNIA

Q: What do you know now as an artist that you didn't know ten years ago?

A: I used to think I was going to run out of ideas. I thought there was a limit to my making and that I needed to hoard projects or words or supplies because my creativity was going to dry up. What I have come to understand is that making breeds making. Creativity is a muscle and the more you use it, the stronger it gets. My ideas should be used and shared and celebrated, never saved up.

Q: If you could give moms who long to create as they raise their children a word of advice or encouragement, what would it be?

A: Let them see you making. You may be operating as if your creative work is something you need to make time for outside of time with your kids. You may be trying to hoard the minutes after they go to bed or while they are at school or during naps. That's okay! But so many of the minutes with your kids are a good time for you to practice creativity too. My girls have grown up watching me knit and sew and cross-stitch and throw pottery and paint our walls and build displays and rearrange furniture. They have seen me make mistakes and cry in frustration and throw out my garbage work. They have seen me start over and turn a pile of fabric into a finished dress and dance around the house with joy when my idea becomes reality. I am so glad they have seen it all.

When we consistently show up to our creative work, the end result far surpasses any single masterpiece we finish. All of those hours co-creating with God culminate in a life filled to the brim with wonder and curiosity and awe, a front row seat to the mystery of God. Our end result is a sharpened faith, a deeper reverence, a heightened ability to, as Brian Doyle says, "detect God's fingerprints."[2]

This is why, like Noah, we keep going. This is why we keep showing up, even when we don't feel like it. This is why we stay disciplined. Because every day that we show up to the ark, the blank page, the roll of film, the pile of flour—we are accepting an invitation to make something meaningful, all the while clinging to God's promises.

IN *THE ARTISAN SOUL,* Erwin Raphael McManus offers his own version of tough love: "We hope that discovering our talents, and even our calling or purpose, will lead us to effortless success. I would propose that the exact opposite is true: if God created us to be successful at something, then he has called us to work hard at it."[3]

This is the unsexy part of pursuing our creative gifts—the showing up, the consistency, the hard work. We'd much rather talk about the magic, the brilliant ideas in the shower, the holy moment we create an exquisite piece of art that later inspires the world. Who wants to talk about discipline? *Ugh!*

Not only is discipline mundane and tedious, it can also be intimidating, especially when we adopt an all-or-nothing approach.

I know this because I try to overhaul my entire life every six months. Usually, one little thing will push me over the edge, like finding a carton of rotting fruit in the refrigerator, or discovering a huge medical bill that is past due. Suddenly I am spinning around the house like a hurricane. *We need weekly budget meetings! A robust meal plan! A system for checking the mail! And while we're at it, let's start exercising six days a week! WE NEED TO GET OUR LIVES TOGETHER!*

I'm sure this doesn't shock anyone, but overhauling my entire life has never worked. Not once. Similarly, if I haven't written in a while, I can't start writing ninety minutes a day, seven days a week. The jump is too big, the mountain too high.

Instead, we must start small. It's okay to begin with tiny, doable steps. Clear off the desk. Organize the paints. Charge the camera battery. Print the recipe. Take the flute out of the closet and put it in plain sight. What does a small beginning look like for you?

I'll tell you one of my biggest creative secrets: a phone timer and peanut butter cups. When I really, really, really do not feel like writing, I set the timer on my phone, and I place a peanut butter cup on my desk. After I write for forty-five minutes, the timer buzzes, and I get a treat. Yes, like a pet. Or a potty-training toddler.

I am not above bribing myself, is what I am trying to say.

Maybe you need a bribe, too. Maybe you need the promise of a second cup of coffee. Maybe you want to set loftier goals and prizes, like a trip to the art gallery after you finish ten paintings. Or a new cookbook after you try a certain number of online recipes.

I'll never forget hearing the parenting advice "sleep begets sleep" and thinking, *What a load of crap.* The joke was on me though, because any time I'd purposely keep my baby awake (you know, so he'd be *extra* tired!)—ten out of ten times, that strategy blew up in my face.

The less my baby slept, the less my baby slept. I still can't make sense of this truth—it seems to defy logic—but I guess I'm here to tell you the experts were right. Sleep really does beget sleep.

That same rule applies to creativity, too. The more we create, the more we create.

The more we write, the more stories we think of. The more photographs we take, the more memories we seek to preserve. Even better? This rule often transcends genres. The more we sing, the more we dance. The more we bake, the more parties we host. Our writing can inspire our photography, and our photography can inspire our home decor, and our home decor can inspire our hospitality, and on and on and on.

Creativity begets creativity.

All of that showing up pays off in the end. All of the hard work reaps its own reward.

A FEW YEARS AGO, Brett and I bought a fixer-upper.

I immediately fell in love with the natural light and spacious backyard, which made it easy to overlook the toaster in the wall, the hot pink wall paneling, and the ceiling that leaked every time it rained.

We moved in and started watching YouTube videos like a couple of dummies who had never stripped wallpaper before. (No really, we had never stripped wallpaper before.) We ripped up the blue carpet and hired someone to scrape the popcorn ceilings. Sadly, the toaster in the wall (hello, fire hazard!) had to go as well, even though I secretly wanted to keep it as a party trick. *Come on over neighbors, BYO Pop-Tarts!*

The more we fixed, the more problems we found. The electricity only worked half the time. The dishwasher was busted. Every time we cut into a wall, we'd find a ball of wires carelessly crammed inside, like candy wrappers shoved in the back of a kid's underwear drawer.

Is it just me, or do Chip and Joanna make this stuff look easy? They're always like, *Let's buy this adorable dilapidated house for $150,000 and walk through it with a glass-half-full attitude!* Next thing you know, the house is covered in shiplap and forty throw pillows and looks brand new. I am fully aware they have an actual crew of contractors and designers and plumbers and electricians at the helm, but I still think they make home renovation look too easy.

But don't we love makeover shows like that? We love to see a good before and after, a quick swipe-right comparison. We don't care as much about the middle: living in constant disarray, fighting over paint colors, the compromises and sacrifices, the mistakes and

The more we show up to our creativity, even when we don't feel like it, the more we start to view all of life as a creative act.

corrections, the leaks, the mold, the dwindling bank account, the things we learn about ourselves when nothing is going according to plan.

We just want to see the tour of the ramshackle house, and then the grand finale once the makeover is complete.

I'm not one to talk. I'm tempted to beg for a shortcut all the time. I often wish I had a red plastic "easy" button, like those Staples commercials. I wish I could outsource potty training, sleep training, all the other trainings. I wish I could take a simple writing workshop and boom, become a better writer overnight.

That's not how any of this works, though, is it?

Your kids don't magically wake up potty trained at two and a half years old. You can't make over an entire fixer-upper in fourteen days (unless you're Chip and Joanna). You don't learn how to dance, knit, or write poetry in your sleep. You gotta put in the work.

Showing up is half the battle, but showing up is where we get better. This is where we grow in our craft. This is where we learn commitment and stamina and how to hold ourselves accountable. This is where we get to practice courage and tenacity. This is where we learn grit, perseverance, how to fall down and how to get back up. This is where we establish rhythms and routines, where all of our tiny steps become habits over time.

We live in a culture obsessed with final products, but the middle matters greatly. The showing up, the discipline, the putting your butt in the chair—*this is where the magic happens*. The more we show up to our creativity, even when we don't feel like it, the more we start to view all of life as a creative act.

Get your peanut butter cups ready, and you'll see what I mean.

On a day when you are not in the mood to create, set a timer and create anyway. Put a treat on your desk, if you wish.

JOURNALING PROMPT

Using the children's book *If You Give a Mouse a Cookie* as inspiration, write about a time one creative act led to another, and another, and another.

10

GO WHERE
THE LIGHT IS

When I ask my client what time of day the light is best in her house, she responds with an answer no photographer wants to hear: "Honestly, the light in my house isn't great."

When I get to her house, I do a quick scan of the layout, and, much to my dismay, she is correct. There isn't much light. Both the baby's room and the master bedroom are dark, even with all of the shades and curtains pulled open. Rays of sunlight radiate through the kitchen, but I cannot possibly photograph a newborn around a microwave and make that look . . . *natural*.

I sneak down the hall, desperately seeking a solution, and notice a barely ajar door to a room I haven't seen yet. I slowly push it open and almost gasp in delight. A window! The mom meets me in the hallway, quickly apologizing for the mess, the cluttered desk, the boxes of miscellaneous items sitting on the floor.

I hadn't even noticed.

"This used to be our office, but it's kind of a catchall room now," she explains, blushing.

I barely hear her as my eyes lock on the cream-colored tufted day-bed sitting underneath the window. Sunshine cascades through the plastic blinds, creating zebra-like stripes of majestic light across the cushion.

"Can we take pictures in *here*?" I ask her. "The light is perfect!"

She wavers for a moment, bouncing her new baby back and forth in her arms. I can tell she doesn't want to take pictures in this room. I can tell I'm going to have to convince her.

"Let's move some stuff around," I coax. "What if we get rid of the beanbag and slide the desk toward the door to make more space?"

Her husband plays a quick game of furniture Tetris with me, moving bulky items out of the room and stacking cardboard boxes in the corner. Five minutes later, we are staring at a simple bed in front of a bright window, and I am in photographer heaven.

A few minutes into the shoot, I'm clicking my shutter button with confidence, moving around the room energized and inspired. The mom starts to relax. She sees what I see: her precious family, posed against a simple backdrop, enveloped in sunshine and love. I photograph the entire session in what started as a messy office.

Before I leave, the mom confesses with a hint of surprise in her voice, "I would have never thought to take pictures in that room."

I smile, thank her for trusting me, and offer up a photography tip on my way out the door. "If you want to take beautiful pictures, you have to go where the light is."

I PICKED UP A FANCY CAMERA for the first time in 2009. The more I learned about photography, the more enamored I became with the way light shifted and changed throughout the day, illuminating different areas of my house. I felt like a child who had just stumbled across a long-lost toy hiding underneath the bed. *Was this really here the whole time?*

Brett and I have moved three times since I became interested in photography, and light is now the first thing I notice when we walk through a house. Whether we're renting or buying, I can look past a lot—dated kitchen cabinets, a cramped layout, grimy bathrooms with salmon-colored tiles up the wall—but nothing sends me running out of a house faster than a lack of windows.

Most days I follow beams of sunshine around my house like a cat. Light makes me feel warm, content, safe. Light fills me up like a four-course meal. Light makes me notice things I wouldn't normally notice, like the way the shadows from the backyard maple trees dance across our living room wall when it's windy. Light draws me in like a magnet, urging me to pick up my camera and document every facet of its magic, as if whispering, *Can you even believe how beautiful I am?*

I'm reminded of the way Presley loves to grab my hand and physically pull me around the house. "Come wif me, Momma," she says, dragging me to the trampoline, to her reading corner, to the parade of doodled papers she's lined up along the floor. With every tug of her tiny hand, she pulls me deeper into her world, her mind, her joy, toward whatever lights her up.

Inspiration pulls us in the same way—a holy invitation of sorts, beckoning us toward beauty and grace, hope and awe.

A FEW YEARS AGO, Brett and I decided to embark upon a popular eating plan that involved cutting out sugar, dairy, grains, and alcohol for a month.

At the time, between stressful jobs and two small children, our collective nutrition had fallen by the wayside. We ate tons of takeout, tons of cereal, and tons of "quick fix" meals in the name of survival. We constantly felt tired and sluggish, often relying on caffeine and sugar to get us through our afternoon slumps. I got headaches almost every day. *Something* had to change.

And, well, what do you know? As it turns out, dipping animal crackers in a jar of Nutella every afternoon makes me feel pretty terrible, both physically and mentally. And, as it turns out, eating fruits, vegetables, and real, unprocessed food makes me feel pretty great, on all accounts.

My body went from feeling lethargic and weak to energized and strong. My mind went from fuzzy and overworked to sharp and alert. I have never been more aware of the connection between what I eat and how I feel than I was at the end of those thirty days.

As the saying goes—garbage in, garbage out.

The quality of *output* is determined by the quality of *input*.

I don't know about you, but I can easily live in denial about cause and effect. I love to pretend I can eat whatever I want without

> If we want to *create* inspiring art, we have to *consume* inspiring art. We have to go where the light is, toward what is lovely, toward what makes us feel alive.

bloating, headaches, or regret. Likewise, I love to pretend I can fill myself up with reality TV and social media and still turn around and produce high-quality creative work. But in the same way a runner does not eat an entire pizza before a marathon, I cannot possibly spend eight hours watching *The Real Housewives* and then sit down to create a profound, well-written story.

Input affects output, for better and for worse.

Good writers read good books. Good musicians listen to music that's stood the test of time. Good painters study the masters. Artists who take their craft seriously know how to bathe themselves in beauty, in stories and lyrics and photos that take their breath away.

If we want to *create* inspiring art, we have to *consume* inspiring art. We have to go where the light is, toward what is lovely, toward what makes us feel alive.

WHEN I WAS A YOUNG MOM, I couldn't help but notice an underlying, persistent negativity surrounding the topic of motherhood. From blogs and online forums to social media and TV shows, every type of medium seemed full of the same miserable caricatures. Moms were exhausted and irritable. Covered in spit-up. They were always yelling at their children and snapping at their husbands. They missed their pre-baby clothes, their pre-baby bodies, their pre-baby lives.

The more negativity I consumed, the more I struggled to separate what I read and what I watched from my real, true feelings about motherhood.

Have you ever been part of a conversation where a complaint becomes contagious, or martyrdom becomes a password at the door? Negativity can easily turn into a rash we can't stop picking at, one that spreads. As a new, impressionable mom, I noticed how quickly a steady diet of bitterness and resentment produced those same attributes in my own heart.

I'm learning that just as a well-nourished creative pours better work into the world, a well-nourished mother pours better love into her family.

When we take a holistic approach to filling ourselves up physically, mentally, emotionally, and spiritually—*everyone around us benefits*. When we fill up our bodies and minds and hearts with what is good and pure and true, that *input* creates better *output*.

As mothers, we pour out daily: food, affection, discipline, grace, connection. We feed our children, clothe them, hug them, disciple them. And then we get up the next day and do it all over again. If we want to show up to this work filled to the brim with love and patience, we have to make sure we are replenishing ourselves with the right kind of input.

Good input might look like reading instead of scrolling, or feeding ourselves a real lunch instead of a handful of Goldfish crackers. Good input could be signing up for a Bible study, or investing in a small group of women who speak life over our mothering. Good input could be taking a shower, or taking a nap, or taking a walk, intentionally giving our bodies and minds what they need to thrive.

While I'm no longer a new, impressionable mom, I still see the "motherhood is so hard" narrative everywhere. And motherhood *is* hard. I'm not suggesting this holy work is easy, or that we shouldn't speak honestly about the ways motherhood brings us to the end of ourselves.

But we are not going to love motherhood more if we surround ourselves with people and media and influences that constantly complain about it.

Even in motherhood, we can go where the light is.

I USED TO THINK OF CREATIVITY solely in terms of output, like beaded jewelry and wall hangings, or flower arrangements and hand-spun pottery.

I never gave as much thought to input, to the inspiration that fills us up *before* we create. But creativity is both a give and a take, a balancing act between consumption and creation. If anything, the more I create, the more I'm learning to see tangible output as only a small fraction of the story.

Creativity is far more than the act of making and producing art. Creativity is casting a vision. Creativity is cultivating a heart that beats for beauty, glory, and splendor. Creativity is tuning in to the sparks of inspiration popping in our minds like fireworks. Creativity is the art of paying attention and using our senses: tasting chocolate, smelling pine needles, listening to a saxophone player serenade commuters in a train station.

I think we're often tempted to minimize the importance of good input, or blow it off entirely. Because if we only have an hour to create, we'd rather have something to show for ourselves, and our time, at the end of the day.

But rich, vibrant art is only born out of a rich and vibrant inner life.

Makoto Fujimura proposes that beauty is not necessary for survival, but beauty is necessary for our flourishing.[1] Surely this sentiment can be applied to those of us examining our input to output ratios. Are we simply surviving as artists, churning out uninspired work for the sake of churning it out? Or are we flourishing as artists, taking the time to pause, see, taste, hear, and be pulled toward the light?

If we indeed create more beautiful and meaningful art when we draw inspiration from a deep, prosperous well, we must view the act of nourishing our creative souls as a vital part of the creative process.

This is good news, and a form of permission, for the creative who is stuck. You might be in a season right now when you are not making anything. Your journals are empty. Your canvases are blank. Your sewing machine is collecting dust. Maybe you're in the thick of a difficult circumstance you have no control over. Maybe you're grieving some kind of loss, or intentionally pausing to figure out your next steps. Maybe you're just feeling down, self-critical, and frustrated with your creative life.

KRISTIN YOUNG

PHOTOGRAPHER, WRITER

@KRISTINMYOUNG

CHARLOTTE, NORTH CAROLINA

Q: How does your faith inspire or affect your creative work?

A: I started seminary four years ago. At that time, I thought I had to put my camera on the shelf to pursue my passion for theology. I felt as though the two could not coexist. However, I learned through taking a theology and art class that God is the original creative Creator. Art is an extension of Him in us. All we must do is look in the mirror to see the genius of God's creation. In photography and life, finding the light, or Light, is paramount. I try to capture that Light of the soul in everyone I photograph.

I invite you to reframe this season from one of lost art to one of found art. A season of more input and less output. A season to receive rather than give. Pick up a good book. Scour YouTube until you find an interview with your favorite comic, actress, or musician. Take a stroll through a botanical garden. Watch a sunset. Give yourself permission to seek out beauty, to feast on it for a while.

There is a time to pour ourselves out into our art, but there is also a time to refill the well.

"OOOOOOH, LOOK AT *DAT ONE*, MOMMA!" Presley points at a hanging plant perfectly poised over what appears to be a fairy garden. I'm not sure if she's enchanted by the plant or the tiny wooden fairies. Probably both.

Q: What do you know now as an artist that you didn't know ten years ago?

A: I realized that opening a business does not validate me as a photographer. What makes me a photographer is that I go out to shoot and make pictures. I have found more value and joy having personal projects that I invest in because they interest me or are an extension of me. Unapologetically shooting what I love and what matters to me is more important now. You will see lots of images of my family, as they are my muses and favorite subjects.

It's Wednesday morning, and Presley should be in preschool right now. Due to a COVID exposure, her classroom's been shut down for ten days. Just like that, two weeks of (already limited) childcare, *poof*, gone.

I'll admit, I did not have a good attitude about this change of plans. I arrange all of my meetings, and all of my deadlines, around twelve precious hours of childcare each week. I know I am not the only mother who feels irritable and exhausted from all the pivoting and scrambling and coming up with plan B, plan C, plan D, plan E.

I had a laundry list of tasks to accomplish today, but Presley is practically attached to my leg, so here we are at the nursery instead, buying plants in an attempt to feed my soul. At home, I head into the backyard to dig my hands in the earth while a single tear rolls down my cheek. I lay everything down, again—all my expectations, all the things not in my control—for what feels like the millionth time during this pandemic.

I turn on the Avett Brothers and sing along as dirt collects under my fingernails.

When the last plant is potted, I go inside and wash my hands and decide on a whim to make chocolate chip cookies. I set aside half the dough so the next time I am forced to pivot, I will have a gift waiting for me in the freezer. I pick my boys up from school and take them straight to the library, because—along with cookies and plants—good stories always remedy a bad day.

I make a mental list of small graces. The delight of licking cookie dough off the spoon. The calming sound of wind blowing through the backyard trees. The way Presley said, of her own accord, in the middle of the succulent aisle, "Momma, I luv spending time wif you."

During naptime, when I finally have the chance to work, I give myself permission to ignore the emails and leave the dishes. I fight the temptation to curl up with *The Real Housewives* and curl up with a Brian Doyle book instead.

Two pages in, he writes, "Thrashing toward light with a sharp pen is what writers do."[2]

I like the quote so much, I copy it down in my notebook.

I did not cross a single thing off my to-do list today. But I spent time with my daughter, put my hands in the dirt, and made cookies for my family. I listened to music I love, felt sunshine on my skin, and read a good book. I added beauty and life to my backyard, a gift we'll continue to enjoy for months, maybe even years to come.

I guess you could say I found light in lots of places.

CREATIVE EXERCISE

Pay attention to the light in your house. Where does it start? Where does it end? How does it move? Notice the way light trickles across the floor, climbs up the walls, bounces off the mirrors. Notice when you can see dust in the air, when the glow shifts from bright to dim. Spend a day "chasing light" in your house with your camera. Take pictures throughout the day as you go where the light is.

JOURNALING PROMPT

Write about a time you experienced a beacon of light amidst a season of darkness. Or consider a place or circumstance in your life right now that feels dark. Is there a way you could infuse light into it?

11

NOTHING IS WASTED

I am a New Year's girl through and through. Give me all the fresh calendars, new planners, and blank slates. I am here for all of it, especially the goal setting.

This year, on January 1, I set out to learn how to shoot film.

I had never shot film before, unless you count my Instax Polaroid camera, which, for reference, my kindergartner knows how to use. When I say I started from scratch, I mean it took me thirty minutes and two YouTube videos to figure out how to even load the film in the camera.

Any self-taught photographer will tell you: research and tutorials are good and useful, but the best way to learn how to take pictures is to *take pictures*. Lots and lots and lots of pictures. Digital photography, of course, is built for this method of learning. With a digital camera, you can take three thousand bad pictures in the name of practice, and instantly delete them.

Film, though, is different.

I forgot learning a new skill takes practice, patience, perseverance. I forgot the beauty of making mistakes and learning from them.

With film, every photo costs you something. The film itself costs money. Getting the film developed costs even more money. I can practically hear the *cha-ching* every time I hit the shutter button.

You can imagine how disheartening it would be to finally receive your scans back and realize that more than half your images didn't turn out the way you'd hoped. Some are out of focus. Some are underexposed. And, worse, almost all of the blame can be attributed to user error.

The first time I received film scans back, I sighed in relief. Not every picture was terrible, which is what I had expected. In fact, some of the images were—*dare I even say it?*—good. But then I got the second batch of photos back. And the third. And the fourth. And if I was improving at all, I couldn't see any progress.

For every roll of thirty-six shots, I liked maybe ten of the photos. The other twenty-six? Garbage. As I stared at my computer screen analyzing all my errors, one looming thought hovered over me: *what a waste.*

What a waste of time.

What a waste of money.

What a waste of effort.

Logically, I knew I wasn't going to become the next Annie Leibovitz overnight (or ever), but I still berated myself for every costly mistake, for all the waste involved in this new, expensive, time-consuming hobby of mine.

I forgot learning a new skill takes practice, patience, perseverance. I forgot the beauty of making mistakes and learning from them. I forgot the concept of a learning curve, and that I was still at the bottom of the graph.

I forgot to give myself grace as a beginner.

I forgot good things take time.

TWELVE YEARS AGO, I started a health blog.

(I will pause here and let you laugh. It *is* funny. Me, the girl who regularly eats cereal for dinner, writing about health. *Hardy har har.*)

While I quickly realized I didn't love writing about nutrition and exercise, I *did* enjoy writing on the Internet. So, I ditched the health blog and created a personal blog called Where My Heart Resides (a name which, now that you mention it, is perfectly suited for a teenage girl's diary).

I changed the name a few years ago (ashleegadd.com, so original!), but the space is, more or less, the same. A few months ago, I set out to give my blog a makeover and had to go through the entire archive to re-categorize posts to work with my new template.

Reading through a dozen years' worth of old blog content was—*how shall I say this delicately?*—absolutely horrifying. It took every ounce of willpower in my body not to delete 75 percent of the posts. I spent an entire afternoon skimming through stories I wrote when I was twenty-five, twenty-six, twenty-seven years old, cringing so hard my face physically hurt. I wanted to grab my younger self by the shoulders and yell, *WRITE BETTER THAN THIS. BE better than this!*

People keep telling me the personal blog is dead. That blogging is a waste of time, that the world is moving to newsletters and TikTok now. It would be easy to buy into that narrative, just as it would be easy to look back on this blog I've faithfully kept for twelve whole years, a blog that literally costs me money, that hardly anyone reads, and write the whole thing off as a waste.

But I can't seem to do that.

My personal blog was my first foray into telling stories on the Internet. Today I do that in other ways—through essays for Coffee + Crumbs, through Instagram, through newsletters and podcasts.

But I believe there is something to be said for humble beginnings. My personal blog is where I first learned the sacred practice of creating art and releasing it into the world. My personal blog is where I learned to write honestly, even when I didn't write well. (And trust me, I didn't.)

Every lousy word I wrote back then set me on a path to where I am today. To the words I wrote yesterday and the words I will write tomorrow. As embarrassed as I may feel about my personal blog posts circa 2009, as my good friend Katie says, I wouldn't be *here* without *there*.

IN THE GOSPEL OF JOHN, there's a story about a large crowd following Jesus that becomes hungry (hey moms, sound familiar?). A boy appears with two fish and five loaves of bread, and after giving thanks for it, Jesus feeds five thousand people.

I've always loved this story because it reminds me of what God can do with our scraps, our meager efforts, our humble offerings. But I recently read this account again, and one verse in particular caught my eye.

John 6:12 says, "And when they had eaten their fill, he told his disciples, 'Gather up the leftover fragments, that nothing may be lost.'"

At the very least, you'd assume figuring out what to do with the leftovers would be someone else's job. *Philip? Andrew? Hello? Jesus handled catering, the least you can do is be in charge of cleanup.*

But no. Jesus is the one who tells them to gather the fragments.

Because with Him, nothing is ever wasted.

Three kids in, I'll confess: I often struggle to see the value in the everyday, mundane minutes. When my kids stroll lazily to the car pick-up line after school, sometimes I want to scream out the window,

"YOU'RE WASTING MY TIME!" When I read a chapter book aloud before bed and my boys cannot answer a single question about the story, it feels like I wasted fifteen minutes of my evening. Do not even get me started on how many times I have vacuumed under the kitchen table only to find a hodgepodge of fruit snacks and cracker crumbs mere minutes later. Constantly, I fight the temptation to throw my hands in the air and yell, "Why do I bother with any of this?!"

Why do I bother cleaning my house when my children wreck it minutes later?

Why do I bother making this food nobody wants to eat?

Why do I bother reading to my boys when they don't appear to be listening?

A while back, we were all in the car and somehow the topic of superheroes came up. I tried to listen to the dialogue between Everett and Carson, giving the occasional *mm-hmm* of pretend interest. I asked who the "best" hero was, fully prepared to fake enthusiasm at the audio dissertation of Marvel characters that would surely come next. But that's not what happened.

Instead, Everett said, "Jesus. Jesus is the biggest hero."

We hadn't been talking about Jesus. We had been talking about Spiderman and Captain America. But in that moment, Everett made a connection to something we've said countless times, something we've read in the *Jesus Storybook Bible* over and over again: Jesus is always the hero. He's the hero of every story, every time.

Pretty soon they were back to Marvel characters, debating the merits of Thor and someone else I can't remember. But that simple answer reminded me of every prayer we've prayed, every Bible story we've read, every church service we've managed to attend. It reminded me of how many times I've wondered if anything we say is sinking in.

That day in the car, in a simple conversation about superheroes, God reminded me nothing is wasted.

Those water bottles you're filling up a dozen times a day? The diapers you're changing? They matter. The minutes you spend rocking your baby in the middle of the night, comforting your child after a rejection at school, whispering prayers before bed—those matter, too. With Him, not one ounce of these daily acts of love, of faith, of sacrifice, of mothering, is wasted.

Because our God is not a God of waste. Scripture tells us, *"In all things* God works for the good of those who love him, who have been called according to his purpose."[1] He takes every situation in our lives and knows exactly what to do with it, like a chef preparing a grand meal where every single ingredient is used to its full potential. *Gather up the leftover fragments, that nothing may be lost.* God doesn't waste mediocre moments. God doesn't waste pain or joy, failure or delight. He doesn't waste time, or chances, or opportunities to refine our hearts.

Our God is going to use up every last drop of us, every last second of our life on this earth, every last word in the story He's already written, for a good and glorious purpose, one we might not ever know or see this side of heaven.

We can rest in knowing all these acts of obscurity matter to the One who sees them. Applying Band-Aids to scraped knees. Tying little shoes. Wiping spilled yogurt off the floor, again.

The same is true of our creativity.

Most of our creative process will forever remain unseen. Someone can read a polished essay in six minutes flat, but they'll never know it took the author sixteen hours to write and revise those words. Someone can slip on a handmade dress in an instant, without ever thinking about the hours of labor that went into creating the pattern, choosing the fabric, sewing the stitches.

When it comes to our creative work, no one will ever fully know or appreciate all that goes on behind the scenes: all the pondering, tinkering, experimenting. No one will ever witness every mistake, all the various attempts and drafts, all the broken pieces along the way.

Here's the good news: our Creator invented behind-the-scenes. We are never alone in this work. We can rest in knowing that the unseen hours we spend creating, just like the unseen hours we spend mothering, are never, ever wasted.

ANYONE WHO KNOWS ME, even a little bit, would tell you I am not a hoarder. You know that emoji of the girl with her arms crossed in front of her body? That is me, guarding my front door at all times, not wanting to let *stuff* inside.

Decluttering is one of my favorite pastimes. Picture me, headphones in my ears, singing along to a Spotify playlist while filling up bags of toys, surplus coffee mugs, and kitchen appliances that haven't been used in years. I am smiling, giddy, practically skipping from room to room.

> These candles simply represent time: minutes
> I kept my butt in the chair, minutes I stared at
> the wall, minutes I showed up and wrote terrible
> sentences, minutes I prayed, "God, I need help."

Tra-la-la, what else can I give away today?

(If it weren't for the four additional people living with me, I feel confident I could pull off living in a tiny house. One dresser for my capsule wardrobe. One set of dishes. One tiny desk. I'd probably run into problems with skincare products and books, but a girl can dream, right?)

I share this context with you so you understand just how out of character it is that I became a candle hoarder while writing this book.

Years ago, I started lighting a candle every time I sat down to write. This simple practice became part of my writing routine, a Pavlovian trick of sorts, a signal to my brain that it's time to focus. I keep a small collection of candles of varying sizes and styles in the hall closet for this very reason, most of which I've purchased on clearance at Target. Depending on the size, I usually burn through a full candle every four to twelve weeks.

One day, knee-deep in writing my book proposal, a grapefruit candle on my desk took its last breath. The light disappeared. A tiny cloud of smoke rose up in its place. And I just sat there staring at the swirl of smoke, completely mesmerized, suddenly aware of how many hours I had already logged on this book.

Most of my tin candles have a twelve-hour burn time, but the bigger ones—the ones in jars—burn for seventy to eighty hours.

I decided right then, holding the grapefruit candle in my hands, that I would keep every single candle I burned while writing this book.

At the very end, I would take a picture of the used-up candles as a visual representation of every hour I logged wrestling words out of my head and onto these pages.

These candles do not represent a word count, or progress on any given chapter. These candles simply represent time: minutes I kept my butt in the chair, minutes I stared at the wall, minutes I showed up and wrote terrible sentences, minutes I prayed, "God, I need help."

These candles remind me of every quiet morning God met me on these pages. They remind me how much I learned about faith and surrender in the process, even though a good portion of the words I wrote—hours and hours *and hours* of writing—would get cut from this book in the end.

They remind me with God, no minute is ever lost.

They remind me with God, nothing is wasted.

CREATIVE EXERCISE

Purposefully create something that *won't last*. Go outside with your kids and "paint" water on the sidewalk, where it will evaporate minutes later. Or build a sandcastle close enough to the ocean to be swept away with the tide. Shape Play-Doh into masterpieces, and then put it right back in the container.

JOURNALING PROMPT

Write about a time you thought a circumstance would be a waste—of time, money, resources, etc.—but now, looking back, you can see how God wove meaning and purpose into the situation.

12

IT TAKES A VILLAGE

"I do it by *self!*" Presley insists, furrowing her brows. We've just returned home from a walk around the neighborhood, and she is determined to climb out of the stroller without help. I take a deep breath and position my body next to the front wheel as a human guardrail in case she falls.

After what feels like two hours, the soles of her sandals finally hit the pavement.

"I did it!" she says, boasting with pride.

This is our new routine: my daughter refuses help at least seven times an hour, and then looks to me for immediate approval and praise when she finally manages to do whatever task she set out to do. It's incredible, really. I always thought I'd be responsible for my kids until the age of eighteen, but at a whopping two years old, apparently Presley no longer requires assistance with any aspect of her life. She can eat an apple by herself (as evidenced by the half-dozen apples left all over the house with exactly three teeth marks in each one), she can get into the car seat by herself (takes four times longer than climbing out of the stroller, in case you were wondering), and she can even wash her hands (sort of), that's right, you guessed it—*all by herself!*

I guess my work here is done? What on earth will I do with all this free time?!

Every time she says, "I do it by self!"—a wave of déjà vu hits me. My boys exercised their independence around this same age, too. At first, I found their self-sufficiency endearing. Liberating, even. *Wow, they really CAN carry the train bin/brush their teeth/climb into the trampoline by themselves.* Other days, the stubborn dedication to putting on their own shoes when we were already running fifteen minutes late was enough to make me yell, "NO YOU CAN'T!"

These days, my daughter swells with pride each time she puts a banana peel in the garbage, quickly looking at me for a reaction.

"Look, Momma! I frow it away by self!"

I plaster a smile on my face with an enthusiastic nod and a sincere "Good job, babe!"—as if she's just won the National Spelling Bee and not thrown away a piece of trash. As a parent, I know part of my job is to encourage independence. My husband and I are raising children who will eventually become adults, and it would be nice if they could brush their own teeth and tie their own shoes and (dreaming big) go to the bathroom unassisted someday.

At the same time, Presley's sudden obsession with doing things by herself saddens me, because it was only six months ago that she defaulted to the opposite: "Momma, I need help."

I don't know exactly when things shifted, but now every time I ask her if she needs help, the answer is no. And not just no. Certainly not "No, thank you."

It's more like "*NO!!!!!*"

She refuses my assistance with passion, practically offended by the offer. How dare I ask if she needs help? She is two whole years old! She knows how to do things! She is strong! And smart! And capable!

I often roll my eyes at my daughter's newfound self-reliance, even though, deep in my bones, I know exactly how she feels.

I know because I used to be just like her.

Sometimes, I still am.

THE FIRST TIME I RECEIVED an invitation to playgroup, I packed an embarrassing number of supplies for the occasion: snacks, backup snacks, sippy cup, diapers, wipes, change of clothes, backup change of clothes, butt cream, sunscreen, and three different kinds of teething ice packs.

(I was a first-time mom—*you know how we do*. I rarely left the house without a full diaper bag prepared for everything short of a zombie apocalypse.)

My new friend, Christina, opened the door and whisked me inside. *That's Lee! And that's Caelin! And this is Sarah!* A group of chatty moms sat on the carpet surrounded by adorable babies and drool-covered toys. I took a seat on the floor and introduced myself with a nervous smile.

At the end of the morning, they invited me to join them the following week, so I did. Then I showed up the week after that, and the week after that. Before I knew it, I had unofficially become a member in their club.

Every Thursday morning, we rotated hosting playgroup in our homes. Whoever hosted would provide scones and coffee for the moms, goldfish crackers and juice boxes for the kids. Some days we'd sprawl out on the carpet, swapping stories over the noise of half a dozen babbling children. Other days, we'd sit outside in the sunshine, monitoring babies in swim diapers splashing in a blow-up pool.

Eventually our toddlers turned into preschoolers, and, with time, we added half a dozen more babies to the posse. Oddly enough, as my children and friendships continued to grow, a funny thing happened to my diaper bag: *it shrunk.*

This is, of course, bound to happen as your kids get older. But another shift was happening, too. Not with my kids, but with me. As I built trust with these fellow moms, I realized I didn't need to show up to playgroup stocked with sunscreen and butt cream and emergency Band-Aids, because the hostess had all that stuff on hand and would surely cover me if I needed something. I didn't need to keep showing up to playgroup with half a baby registry slung over my shoulder.

Over time, I learned to accept someone else's spare Boogie Wipes, someone else's bug spray. Over time, I learned to be okay with my kid eating Puffs out of someone else's container.

Eventually, I stopped bringing a diaper bag altogether.

WHEN I FIRST BEGAN DABBLING IN WRITING and photography, I locked arms with Google as my one and only business partner. Who needs a mentor when you have YouTube? Who needs to ask a friend for help when you can ask a forum on the Internet?

I consulted my BFF, Google, on all kinds of things:

How to start a blog

How to use a DSLR camera

How to edit videos with iMovie

How to make graphics for Instagram

Anytime I couldn't figure something out, I simply took to the Internet for five hours until I found an answer. At the time, my entire creative process could be summed up like this: Girl Hunches over Laptop, Swears by Trial and Error and Copious Amounts of Googling.

Back in those early years, I created mostly in a vacuum. I wrote by myself, blogged by myself, took pictures by myself. People occasionally offered feedback on my art, sure, but behind the scenes, I operated as an independent party of one, like a single rider on a roller coaster. For the longest time, I thought that's how creative people worked, in total and complete isolation (you know, cabin-in-the-woods style).

> I willingly chose confinement over community because creating alone seemed like a safer bet. Less risky, less vulnerable.

If anyone had even tried to help me back then, I probably would have channeled some rendition of my daughter's favorite line: *"No! I do it by self!"*

I willingly chose confinement over community because creating alone seemed like a safer bet. Less risky, less vulnerable. By creating in a silo, I could keep all my fears and doubts and insecurities locked up in my chest, right where I preferred them to stay.

Google never laughed at me (that I knew of).

I had nothing to lose.

Although, as I would later learn, I had nothing to gain, either.

TWO YEARS AGO, I approached three friends about starting a mastermind group. At the time, we all had tiny dreams of writing books, and I figured it would be helpful to share resources and hold each other accountable as we worked on our individual book proposals.

But shortly after we formed the group, we realized what we all *really* wanted was to "level up" in our writing. We agreed to keep chatting about our book dreams, but we also clarified the mission of our mastermind: we wanted to grow as writers, together.

We started a group chat on Voxer, where we began talking every single day. About writing, yes, but about plenty of other things, too. Marriage. Motherhood. Faith. We talked about the ordinary moments of our days, along with critical events happening in the world. With every passing day, and every stitch of conversation, we opened up to one another a little bit more, like a bouquet of freshly cut tulips.

Our nonstop group chat quickly became an essential part of my daily routine. We fell into a rhythm of crying and laughing and praying for each other over Voxer as we folded laundry, walked around our individual neighborhoods, or—my personal favorite—sat in silent cars in grocery store parking lots.

We also began critiquing each other's writing. Every two weeks, we submitted a piece to the group for feedback. We could submit an essay, a newsletter, bits and pieces of our book proposals, anything and everything that needed an extra set of eyes.

One particular month, I confessed my frustration over a piece of writing I had been struggling with, whining melodramatically to the group about how I wanted to bang my head against the wall and throw my computer out the window.

Every day, I had worked on this piece. And every day, I hated it more and more.

After listening to me complain what I can only assume was an excruciating number of times, my friend Katie finally suggested I send the piece to the group "as is."

Sarah and Sonya echoed, "Yeah, just send it to us!"

And while these women had quickly grown into some of my most cherished, dearest, closest friends—the first to hear my tears, my fears, my confessions, my prayer requests—in that moment, I felt like they were asking me to do something completely unreasonable. I felt like they were asking me to show up to a party naked.

I couldn't fathom letting my own mastermind group see my lousy essay in its current state—unfinished, unpolished, un-everything. In a flash, I was transported back to being the mom at the playgroup with the ridiculously stocked diaper bag. *Don't worry about me! I've got this covered! I don't need anything at all!*

Right then and there, I knew I had a choice to make. I could let my friends into my current writing struggle, or I could "do it by self." I could set down my ego and accept the help, or I could continue toiling in isolation.

I cringed when I hit send on the email.

This should come as no surprise: once my mastermind group got their hands on my sub-par, unfinished draft, their feedback instantly made it better. They offered clarity, fresh eyes, and brilliant suggestions on areas I could improve. They asked thoughtful questions and helped me process what I was trying to communicate, so I could identify where I had strayed off course.

My essay became better because of their edits, but the edits aren't what blessed me most. In a moment of despair and frustration, my friends spoke life over me, and over my writing, when I had been tempted to speak death over all of it. Julia Cameron calls these types of friends "believing mirrors"—people who reflect back to us our potential and the potential of our work.[1]

When I was in labor with Carson, there came a moment when I wanted to just . . . *give up*. I had begged for drugs, but they never came. I couldn't take the pain anymore.

At one point, I threw my body back on the bed and yelled, "I CAN'T DO IT!!!!"

In my memory, there is not even a one-second pause between my collapse and every midwife in the room yelling back at me, "YES, YOU CAN!" They believed in me when I couldn't believe in myself.

In *Adorning the Dark*, Andrew Peterson describes community as friends who tell us, *This is worth doing*. He writes: "They look you in the eye and remind you who you are in Christ. They reiterate your calling when you forget what it is. They step into the garden and help you weed it, help you to grow something beautiful."[2]

When I start to get lost, these women help me find my way again. When I break down in tears, as I have done with this group probably more than fifty times, wallowing in my fears, my doubts, my overwhelming insecurities, they pick me up off the floor. They remind me what is true—about me, about God, about this holy work I am pursuing.

And just like a team of midwives, every time I want to quit, every time I say, "I can't do it!"—my friends are right there to remind me, "Yes, you can."

I DID NOT REALIZE how many people I had told I was pregnant until I had to un-tell them all.

"Sad news," I begin to text.

No baby.

Will need a D&C.

I am okay.

Would appreciate your prayers.

Responses barrel in like a flood. Everyone is sorry. Everyone is praying for me. I read text after text in my bed, where my body remains perfectly tucked under a weighted blanket, sandwiched between excessive amounts of pillows and a heating pad. I have made myself a cocoon, a protective shell. I tell everyone I am okay. And I *am* okay. But I am also numb. Empty. Depressed. Anxious. Sad and broken. I am both okay and not okay.

Hours later, flowers appear on the porch. Pizza and pasta and lemonade are delivered like manna at 5:00 p.m. sharp. The next morning, at 7:00, a grocery delivery materializes: muffins, chicken noodle soup, French bread, quesadilla supplies, and ice cream. DoorDash gift cards show up in my inbox. More calls, more texts. *I'm bringing dinner Tuesday. Plan for me to drop off dinner Wednesday. I'll feed you the night of the D&C.*

I don't try to stop any of it.

I simply say, "Okay. Yes. Thank you."

A friend texts that she is going to Target and asks if I need anything. I text her a picture of the single roll of toilet paper in our house

> But God is showing me there is something holy about letting people into your brokenness.

and ask if she can buy me toilet paper. She asks what else I need and I answer sincerely: *A box of Cheez-Its.*

I change out of one pair of sweatpants into another, resisting the urge to apologize to everyone, for everything. *Sorry I'm putting you out. Sorry I have to reschedule that meeting. Sorry I have no energy to talk on the phone.*

With our first pregnancy, Brett and I didn't tell anyone I was pregnant until we had a sonogram in hand. And even then, we only told our parents and close friends for a while. This time around, my fourth time seeing two lines on the stick, I think I told close to forty people I was pregnant before I went to the doctor.

If I had miscarried my first, I am not sure who I would have told. Hardly anyone, probably. I don't like people feeling sorry for me. I don't like to be pitied. I'd rather be the helper than the one being helped, always.

But God is showing me there is something holy about letting people into your brokenness. Just look at my porch, it's practically become hallowed ground. A place to love and be loved. A portal for offerings. A dedicated spot for flowers and food, prayer and cards, toilet paper and Cheez-Its.

ONE DAY AT THE POOL, Presley tried to convince me she could put on her flotation device "by self!" I knew if I tried to help, she'd freak out and scream, so I let her try.

In her defense, she slid the puddle jumper onto her arms just fine. But I knew she'd get stuck with the buckle in the back. So we sat there, she and I, in a two-minute standoff of sorts. Her lips turned down in a pout. She flapped her arms and looked over her shoulder, as if waiting for an answer, or an angel, to appear.

Finally, her body slumped in resignation. Her eyes met mine and she confessed: "I can't do it."

Like her, I, too, used to ask for help as a last resort, only *after* I had exhausted every option on my own. Worn-out, fatigued, and frustrated, I'd eventually slump my shoulders in defeat, just like my daughter at the side of the pool.

We can be quick to roll our eyes when our children say these words, but how many times have we said, *I do it by self!* as mothers? As artists?

How many times have we relied on overpacked diaper bags and our own tired arms, because our pride refused to let anyone help us? How many times have we relied on endless Google searches because our insecurities ran too deep to ask for advice?

How many times have we deliberately chosen to do life alone, simply because we were too afraid to let other people witness our horrendous first attempts, or (gulp, even worse) our parenting mistakes?

How many times have we experienced loneliness for the sake of preserving our own fragile egos? How many people have we left waiting in the wings with their ideas and prayers, their encouragement and advice, their spare Boogie Wipes and love?

Friend, take it from me: *there is a better way.*

We can let people in. We can learn to depend on each other. We can ask for prayer. We can admit Google knows a lot, but he's a pretty crappy friend.

My motherhood village has seen me through multiple pregnancies, a miscarriage, unexpected surgeries for each of my boys. They've dropped off coffee and casseroles and paper bags filled with hand-me-down clothes. They've given me the numbers of their therapists, the

names of their preschools, the tried-and-true potty-training books that worked for them. They've been honest about their guilt, their marital struggles, their postpartum depression—all of which eventually led me to do the same.

Similarly, my creative village has seen me through all kinds of victories and failures. They've spoken life over me, and over my work. They've sent notebooks and quotes, candles and chocolate. They've stepped into battle with me, fighting off lies with prayer and Scripture. They've pushed me to be a better artist, a better writer, not for the sake of accolades or awards, but because they genuinely want me to flourish in my creative gifts. They've encouraged me to rest. They've told me when to delete a comma.

I know some of you are reading this like *great, cool, good for you, but I don't have friends like that.* Dearest reader, a bit of tough love if I may: villages do not create themselves. All friendships start with an invitation, and I will tell you from personal experience that being the inviter is ten times easier than waiting to be invited. I beg you—take this matter into your own hands. Initiate a text thread, a Voxer chain, a Facebook group. Start a book club. Launch your own mastermind. Create your own playgroup. Begin by pouring out what you hope to get back someday: generosity and encouragement, lasagnas and lactation cookies.

You don't have to do any of this—life, mothering, creating—by yourself. In fact, *it's better if you don't*. God has given us one of the best gifts in each other.

CREATIVE EXERCISE

Go first. Pick up the phone. Ask a friend to meet for coffee, or a walk, or a playdate at the park. Host a gathering if you're up for it. (Maybe start a book club? Maybe with this book? *wink*) Plant a seed in a relationship you'd like to see bloom in the future.

JOURNALING PROMPT

Write about a time you felt resistant to accepting help, but finally obliged. What did you learn about friendship and God's grace in the process?

13

REMEMBER TO PLAY

"There's a big present for you under the couch!" Everett tells me a few weeks before Christmas. I look at him skeptically, unsure if he's joking or not. Brett and I agreed not to exchange gifts this year. I, of course, bought him a few small things anyway: a sweater, a book, a pack of specialty hot sauces. But I'm not expecting anything for myself, and certainly not a "big" present.

The only thing I asked for—and I was sort of kidding, but also not kidding at all—was a new vacuum cleaner. (This is how you know you're getting old, when pricey anti-wrinkle creams and vacuum cleaners are at the top of your Christmas wish list.)

The day Everett tells me there is a "big present" under the couch for me, I am convinced he's referring to a cordless vacuum. And I am *thrilled.* Christmas morning, Brett slides a large box over to me. We take turns opening gifts, and when it's finally my turn, I notice a message written in Sharpie marker on the wrapping paper:

To Mommy

We are so lucky to have you. Have some fun this year!

Love, Daddy, Ev, Car-Car & Presley

Suddenly confused, I look quizzically at Brett, who is smiling mischievously. Despite my fondness for keeping a tidy house, I know my husband well enough to know he would never use the word *fun* to accompany a vacuum cleaner.

What in the world is this?

I slowly peel back the wrapping paper to reveal . . . a pink scooter.

I laugh out loud as the memory tumbles back to me. Earlier this year, Everett received a new scooter for his birthday, and on one of our nightly walks around the neighborhood, I had taken it for a spin myself. The second I put my foot on that scooter and pushed off—a sense of pure, unadulterated joy coursed through my body. With sun on my face and wind in my hair, for the first time in a long time, I felt truly spontaneous. Free. Uninhibited. I felt like a kid in the best possible way.

"I want one of these!" I had yelled to Brett, whizzing past him just in time to see Presley staring at me with amusement from the stroller.

I can't believe he actually bought me one.

Have some fun this year.

I slowly run my fingers across the spine of the box, still smiling. I think I will.

I'VE ALWAYS BEEN THE RESPONSIBLE, independent, reliable type. And all my life, I've been praised for these characteristics: for working hard, for pursuing excellence in everything I do, for exceeding other people's expectations. I hate to admit this, but somewhere along the way, I began associating the word *fun* with *leisure* and I began associating the word *leisure* with *lazy*.

At times, I've been quite the martyr about this, throwing myself little pity parties when I witness other people having fun on Instagram. *Must be nice*, I think, pushing my clunky vacuum cleaner around the house, crafting to-do lists in my head.

I was raised with a "work hard, play hard" mentality—in that order, and only in that order. First, you work hard. Then, you play hard. This rhythm led to me viewing play as a reward: something I can only enjoy *after* I hit the word count, clean out the inbox, do x, y, z on the to-do list.

In other words, play is something to be *earned*.

This system worked fine for me as a kid. Once I finished my math homework and completed all of my chores, I could skate in the cul de sac or choreograph a dance routine to the latest Spice Girls song in my bedroom. As a kid, my responsibilities had a clear start, and a clear end, each and every day. Homework, chores, play. Reset the next day. Even in elementary school, I understood the premise of "work hard, play hard."

But then I grew up, got a job, got married, had three kids, and acquired a mortgage. My once simple daily cadence of homework-chores-play morphed into a new, more complicated rhythm, one with layers and nuance and a plethora of grown-up responsibilities.

And, well, I'm not in Neverland anymore. There is always more work to be done, rarely a clear start or end to anything. I am perpetually behind on opening the mail, folding the laundry, scheduling dentist visits. There is always another email to respond to, a writing deadline to meet, pictures to edit.

As an adult, my simple "work hard, play hard" mentality fell by the wayside the minute I realized I couldn't ever see an end to the work. I stopped giving myself permission to play because, try as I might, I never hit the end of the to-do list. I have yet to live one day when I am fully caught up on everything—a day when the essay is finished, the inbox is zero, there is not one dish in the sink or a single sock in the hamper. A day when every single task has a glorious check mark next to it.

Which raises the question: if there is *always* more work to be done, when, exactly, are we allowed to play? If we never get off the hamster wheel of working hard, what happens to our ability to play hard?

What if our resistance to play is actually hindering our art?

Last summer, I read one line in *The Artist's Way* that made me question everything I believed about work and play. Julia Cameron writes, "Creativity lives in paradox: serious art is born from serious play."[1]

In one simple sentence, she flipped the script I'd been reading my entire life. *First,* serious play. *Then,* serious art.

Everything in me wants to fight against that order. The idea of playing as a precursor to engaging in my creative work feels unnatural to me, wrong even, like eating dessert before dinner. But what if Julia's onto something here? Could the act of play, dabbling in fun activities for the sheer sake of delight, propel us forward with more energy and imagination for the serious art we want to make?

For so many years, I have said no to play in the name of taking my craft seriously.

But is it possible to take our craft *too* seriously?

What if our resistance to play is actually hindering our art?

A FEW YEARS INTO PHOTOGRAPHING FAMILIES, I came down with a severe case of the blahs. Suddenly my photos seemed uninspired. Redundant. Stale. All my sessions looked the same—beautiful family in an open field during golden hour. Mom in a long dress, kids in uncomfortable-but-adorable outfits, Dad would rather be anywhere else. *Click click click.* Same candy bribes, same poses, same Lightroom presets.

There was nothing wrong with the images. My clients framed their photos on walls, used them in Christmas cards, shared them on Facebook and Instagram, garnering plenty of positive comments.

But deep down inside, I could not ignore this nagging feeling that I wanted to do something different. I could not ignore this unsettling realization that I was . . . *bored*.

I still wanted to photograph families, but I wanted to try something new, something outside the predictable formula I had been following for years. I kept dreaming of photographing families in their homes, wearing normal clothes, not in fields on the side of the road dressed like a Zara ad. I wanted my sessions to be a little more raw, a little more honest. I craved more blur, more grain, more movement. I wanted to capture the everyday, less-than-perfect moments, the same types of images I loved taking of my own children.

Feeling relatively clear on what I wanted to change, but still confused as to how I could actually do it, I signed up for a photography workshop in San Francisco. A few weeks later, along with a dozen or so other eager students, I pulled up to a charming house on a quiet street lined with bougainvillea.

Over the course of the day, the photographer guided us through a booklet and a series of videos, discussing everything from light and camera settings to forming emotional connections with our clients. She talked about the importance of experimenting, staying curious, and doing "portfolio sessions"—photographing individuals or families for the sole purpose of building up your body of work.

I remember at one point someone asked, "How much should we charge for portfolio sessions?" and the photographer quickly shook her head.

"Money should *never* be exchanged for a portfolio session."

She went on to explain that portfolio sessions are for the photographer, not the client. The second money exchanges hands, the client will have expectations. The second the client has expectations, the photographer loses a sense of creative freedom.

"Portfolio sessions are for *you,* so you can photograph people the way *you* want to photograph them. You can play. Experiment. Try something wild. Try something new."

I came home from that workshop so inspired, I immediately booked portfolio sessions with three families who agreed to let me photograph them in their homes.

I felt awkward and out of my element at the first session. I knew how to photograph families in fields during golden hour, but photographing indoors proved to be trickier. I had to rely on windows for light and get more creative with the way I directed.

Slowly but surely, though, I found a groove. I experimented and tossed out ideas I'd always wanted to try: kids jumping on the bed, playing hide-and-go-seek behind the living room curtains, making a mess in the kitchen baking chocolate chip cookies. By the third portfolio session, I started to feel alive, invigorated, like the freedom had unlocked something in me, like I had finally cracked the code on what kind of photographs I wanted to make. I couldn't help but notice the families seemed more comfortable, more at ease. The dads in particular didn't seem so miserable.

Over the next year, I slowly took down all the photos of families twirling in fields from my photography website. Photos of families in ordinary homes went up in their place: kids brushing their teeth, blowing bubbles in the yard, running through sprinklers. Feeling newly inspired by themes of "home" and "magic in the mundane," I overhauled my entire portfolio. I stopped doing mini sessions, stopped shooting in fields, and got crystal clear on what kind of photography I wanted to pursue.

Looking back, that one workshop in San Francisco completely changed the trajectory of my photography style.

And to think, it all started with one photographer giving me permission to play.

PRESLEY IS OBSESSED WITH MY PHONE CHARGER. Every day, she unplugs it from the wall, wraps it around her shoulders and pretends it's a stethoscope. "Mommy, look! Imma doctor!" She puts the power adapter up to her ear, and the end of the lightning cable on her stuffed animals to listen to their heartbeats.

Sometimes I simply stand by and watch, in awe of the world she's created for herself, nostalgic for the time in my life when I could easily do the same.

When I was a kid, I'd spend a week at my grandparents' house every summer. They lived in a rickety wooden house surrounded by ten acres of dry grass. At one spot in their front yard where the driveway split, there was a huge tree with an oval shape carved into the trunk, probably where a branch had been cut off. That whole section of the driveway became my castle, and I would pretend the carved oval in the tree was a magic mirror. Back at home, my best friend and I would let our Otter Pops completely melt in the plastic tubes, chugging the juice dramatically, pretending to drink potion. We'd host imaginary beauty pageants in the backyard, stuffing water balloons into our bathing suit tops, pretending to have boobs. Every time I got in a pool, I'd swim to the deepest part, dirty blond hair swirling all around me, imagining I was a mermaid. On any given day, I could be a Spice Girl, a queen, a spy.

As a kid, play involved getting lost in my own imagination, dreaming up worlds in my head, and then re-creating those worlds in reality as best I could using the tools at my disposal—nature, toys, whatever I could find.

While I've traded plastic baby dolls for three real kids, and swapped a toy cash register for actual credit card bills, I know this part of my childhood—this living, breathing imagination—still exists within me. I'm still capable of dreaming up worlds in my head.

In *The Artisan Soul*, Erwin Raphael McManus writes: "Imagination always precedes creativity. To engage in the creative act, you must be comfortable working with invisible material."[2]

We can be tempted to downplay imagination as child's play, but imagination is essential to creativity because without it, no art would

> Creativity cannot survive without an active imagination, but this is where so many of us mothers get stuck, in the humdrum of our days.

ever be made. When in doubt, we can look to our Creator as the perfect model of this—Hebrews 11 tells us the entire universe was not made out of what was visible. If God creates by making invisible things visible, we follow that blueprint as well.

We dream *before* we create.

My boys are just now getting into Minecraft, a popular building game. While they are only allowed to play on the weekends, they spend Monday through Friday drafting plans in their sketchbooks like little architects. Their ideas go from their minds to paper, and *then* into the game.

Creativity cannot survive without an active imagination, but this is where so many of us mothers get stuck, in the humdrum of our days. How do we keep our imaginations alive in the throes of scrubbing toilets, prepping for work presentations, cleaning puke out of the carpet?

Could play be the answer?

Play breeds imagination. And imagination breeds play. These two things are vital to living a creative life, but I also believe play and imagination are essential to enjoying motherhood as well.

Adulthood can be a real buzzkill sometimes. Whether you have toddlers or teenagers, whether you work in an office or stay at home, most of us are not gallivanting around the country in a Pinterest-worthy RV crossing inspirational adventures off our bucket lists each day.

I have three darling children and a job I love, but the daily monotony of filling up water bottles and figuring out taxes and checking email and cutting crusts off grilled cheese can give me a serious case of the blahs.

Sometimes I fall into a rut, trapped in what feels like a perpetual Groundhog Day. I remember especially feeling this way in the height of the pandemic, when every day had become the same. Dishes. Laundry. Google Classroom. Working at the same table staring at the same

My children are teaching me that play is not a waste of time.

crumbs on the same floor. I felt restless, anxious, and trapped, like a caged animal desperate to escape. One day, I couldn't take it anymore. I woke up and told my boys we were going to play hooky from Zoom school. On a total whim, I loaded them into the car and started driving to Apple Hill, a group of apple orchards forty miles from our house.

An hour later, we sat down at a picnic table on a grassy hill with three apple cider donuts. I cannot tell you how impossibly refreshing the change of scenery felt—to be outside, to be someplace new, to be breathing different air than the air in our house.

I took over one hundred photos and videos that day, invigorated and inspired by every aspect of our much-needed adventure: the blooming flowers, the scent of fried corn dogs, the taste of fresh apple cider milkshakes. I let my kids feed the ducks. I bought them an over-priced bag of popcorn. I relished being a Yes Mom for the day. I relished being a mom who *plays*.

As mothers and artists, we need adventures from time to time. It's good for us to occasionally orchestrate a day for the sole purpose of sparking our own imaginations, experiencing the glory of creation through sights and sounds, touch and taste.

Sometimes we need to shake things up. There is magic to be found in the mundane, absolutely, but there is also magic galore to be found outside the four walls of our homes. This is your reminder to go outside. Jump on the trampoline. Throw water balloons at your kids. Get in the car, turn the radio all the way up. Roll the windows down, feel the breeze on your face. Step away from the inbox. Step away from the vacuum cleaner.

Play unlocks us, loosens us up. Play grants us permission to try something new for the sake of delight, not mastery. Play brings us back to the little artists we were as kids.

Presley often begs, "Play wif me, Momma!" My boys pull me away from the computer with desperate pleas to judge their Hot Wheels races. While I can't always drop what I am doing, I'm noticing the more I say yes to them, the more I say yes to myself. The more I enter their imaginative worlds, the more I am able to enter my own. My children are teaching me that play is not a waste of time. I'm slowly learning to embrace the idea that play does not have to be earned.

Consider this your friendly reminder: the next time you come down with a case of the blahs, don't be afraid to get your hands dirty. Get yourself a scooter (or borrow one from your kid). Pay attention to your children and follow their lead. Watch them leap around the trampoline and do cartwheels in the grass. Take note of how they turn hot cement into lava, the bottom bunk bed into a puppet stage.

You'll see there is no limit to their imaginations.

Just like there is no limit to yours.

CREATIVE EXERCISE

If you could do anything right now, in the name of play, what would you do? Go treasure hunting at a thrift store? Swim in the ocean? Take a dance class? Make a list of activities or adventures that sound fun to you, and then go do one of those things.

JOURNALING PROMPT

What did play look like for you as a kid? Reflect on your own childhood and write a scene capturing your imagination as a child.

14

FIGHTING
THE GOOD FIGHT

It's 6:00 on a Wednesday evening, and I am sitting in our new "office"—
a standalone shed we recently installed in our backyard.

The first time we saw this house, before it even belonged to us, we
looked past every dilapidated feature—the leaking roof, the stained
carpet, the moldy bathroom—straight through the windows into a
backyard full of promise. The house was small, but the yard was huge.
We began dreaming out loud.

We could build an office out there someday.

Brett started a new remote job the same week a global pandemic
shut down the schools, along with everything else. Like many other
families, suddenly having all of our kids at home 24/7 threw an unexpected wrench into our work-from-home equation. But even without
the glaring challenges of living in lockdown, we quickly realized if we
were *both* going to work from home, indefinitely, we needed to consider bumping the backyard office to the top of our priority list.

Three years of dreaming, six months of planning, and a considerable amount of money borrowed against our house later—here we are, finally turning our office shed Pinterest board into a reality.

Tonight is my first night writing in here, and this moment feels significant. Sacred, almost. I am nestled in a cocoon of four freshly painted walls, experiencing a level of space and privacy I've been severely lacking for over a year.

I light a candle, open up my laptop, and take a deep breath.

Just as I set my hands on the keyboard, a flash of black and red creeps across the left side of my desk. I gasp in horror. It's a bug. A box-elder bug, to be more specific. A bug that, one week ago, I did not know or care anything about. That is, until a few hundred of them flocked to the outside of our shed like fleas on a dog.

Did you know box-elder bugs love maple trees? We have two in our backyard. Did you know they also love warm, bright surfaces, like, *oh, I don't know*, a light grey shed baking in the sun? Did you know they love to reproduce in the early spring? Between our blooming maple trees and the shiny hot walls of our new shed, apparently, we unknowingly fostered a perfect environment for box-elder breeding.

For the past week, every time I've set foot in this shed, I've witnessed no less than fifteen box-elder bugs crawling around on the baseboards, the ceiling, and, yes, my desk.

I wanted everything to be perfect tonight. Instead, I am grossed out. I can practically feel the bugs crawling on me. I am already frustrated and irritable, and I haven't even started writing yet. All the research, labor, planning, and money we've spent on this backyard office—*and now I've got to deal with a plague of insects?!*

As I haul our giant vacuum cleaner through the door, I'm reminded of a line Andrew Peterson writes in *Adorning the Dark*: "If you're called to speak light into the darkness, then believe this: the darkness wants to shut you up."[1]

Tonight, this is how the darkness is trying to shut me up: with bugs, with a distraction, with disgust, with rage vacuuming. The darkness doesn't want me to write beautiful words, to make hope-filled art, to co-create with God. With each and every bug crawling across my desk, it's becoming harder and harder for me to stay focused, disciplined, and inspired.

This is, of course, what the darkness wants—for me to throw my hands up in the air with an exasperated, "I give up!"

A FEW YEARS AGO, I read a caption on author Jennie Allen's Instagram that said, "If you are doing anything of worth, the enemy is doing everything in his power to make you quit."

At times, I have been slow to embrace this notion, because attributing my physical and mental creative struggles to nonspiritual causes feels easier to accept.

Bugs infiltrating my workspace the moment I sit down to write? Coincidence. *Imposter syndrome?* Part of being an artist. *Water pipe breaking in the wall behind my desk, rendering my workspace useless while I spend hundreds of dollars and dozens of hours figuring out how to fix it?* Total fluke. *Massive fight with my husband the day I'm heading out of town for a writing retreat?* Unfortunate timing.

When it comes to my creative victories, though, I am quick to attribute any sign of goodness to the Lord. When I get a great idea in the shower, I thank God for the inspiration. When a kind email hits my inbox at the exact moment I need encouragement, I consider that a divinely timed gift. On the rare occasion writing pours out of me effortlessly, well, any writer would tell you, that is nothing short of a miracle.

So why am I not as quick to attribute the darker stuff, the resistance and stumbling blocks, to a very real enemy waging war against me? Why do I downplay the enemy's involvement in these struggles, in the temptations targeting my specific weaknesses, or the perfectly calculated attacks I sometimes encounter? Why do I insist on chalking *those* up to coincidence?

Just like bugs infesting our workspace, this type of creative spiritual attack can plague our hearts, our minds, our souls. It's in the lies choking us in the middle of the night, whispering we're not qualified to do the holy work God's called us to do. It's in the overwhelming doubt, the crippling fear, the debilitating insecurity. It's in the myth of scarcity, leading us to question whether God actually wants good for us. It's in the temptation to quit, not out of an act of obedience, but as an easy way out. It's in our desire to stay small, not out of humility, but out of fear. It's in our desire to get big, not for the glory of God, but for the glory of ourselves.

The more we set out to infuse the world with beautiful things that reflect life and truth and God's goodness, the more the enemy wants to bring us down. He uses every tool at his disposal to send us spiraling into perfectionism, jealousy, procrastination, conflict. He *wants* us to struggle, to fail, to curl up in the fetal position on the floor and not be able to get back up.

Why? Because mothers and artists are two of the enemy's biggest threats.

ON A CRISP FALL AFTERNOON when my boys were young, I strapped them into our double stroller and ventured out for a walk along the elevated river trail near our house. Once we got to the top of the trail, I stared in awe at the view. The sky looked like an oil painting, a swirly mix of orange and pink and purple hues, with marshmallow clouds added for texture. We completed our normal walk to the bridge and back, but before heading down the path that led to our house, I turned around to snap a quick photo of the sunset.

Click.

As long as I live, I will never forget what I heard next: the sound of a tire rolling on gravel.

In what felt like a fraction of a second, my double stroller tipped over the ledge of the path—heading straight toward the river—with my toddler and newborn strapped inside. I sprinted after them as fast as I could, my arms outstretched, heart pounding out of my chest, not breathing, pleading with God to keep my children safe.

At the bottom of the hill, the stroller crashed into a shrub. The boys were fine, safe, not a scratch on them. I, on the other hand, had taken a fall chasing them down the hill, etching scrapes and cuts into my hands and skin. I walked home covered in bruises and my own blood, but the physical scars were nothing compared to the nightmares that followed.

Even once we were home and safe, any time I'd close my eyes, I'd see a vivid image of the stroller sinking to the bottom of the river with my two children trapped inside. Then I'd see myself diving into the freezing cold water and coming up empty, screaming into the void.

These haunting images terrorized me over and over, like a nightmare I couldn't wake up from. I must have relived that horrendous what-if a thousand times, unable to let go of my own carelessness. *How could I forget to put the brake on the stroller? What kind of mother am I?* At night when I tried to fall asleep, fresh condemnation washed over me. I played that scene on a loop, like a stuck record.

Your children could have died. It would have been all your fault.

Your children could have died. It would have been all your fault.

As I started to inch toward grace, toward mercy, toward better dreams, I could feel another force clawing at my skin, still trying to sink its teeth into me.

I begged God to forgive me. I begged God to help me forgive myself. As I started to inch toward grace, toward mercy, toward better dreams, I could feel another force clawing at my skin, still trying to sink its teeth into me.

That force was going down, but it wasn't going down without a fight.

OUR DAYS AS MOTHERS consist of sacrifice and devotion, holding little bodies until our arms ache, scratching backs until eyelids flutter, preparing snacks again and again. Every act of selfless love we show our children mirrors the heart of God toward us. And every time something reflects God in the world—whether our love or our art—the enemy is going to push back.

The good news? The enemy is always and forever fighting a losing battle.

Priscilla Shirer writes in *The Armor of God* Bible study: "Being a believer doesn't give you immunity from the assaults of the enemy, but it does give you access to the power of the Father—His power to defend you as well as reverse what's been done to you."[2]

At the very beginning of this book journey, I asked ten women to pray over me, and over these chapters as I wrote them. When I first approached this group of women, made up of friends and writing peers scattered across the country, I asked them to be part of my creative village. Within months, though, as resistance started building up— fear, doubt, insecurity, hopelessness—I thought of them less as my village and more as my army.

James 4:7 tells us to resist the devil, and he will flee from us. When Satan tempted Jesus in the wilderness, Jesus didn't hide in response. He didn't sit on a rock and passively wait for God to intervene. He rebuked Satan's lies with Scripture. He fought back. We, too, can fight darkness with light. We, too, can fight the lies of the enemy with truth.

I will confess, sometimes when I'm in the thick of mothering or creating, I too easily forget about my access to the Father. This is, of course, what the enemy wants, isn't it? He wants us to struggle, and then he wants us to believe we can fix everything ourselves. He gets to keep slithering around under the surface, undetected, while we aimlessly take matters into our own hands instead of running to God.

But we cannot fight spiritual battles without spiritual tools.

I'M BACK IN OUR OFFICE SHED TONIGHT. My manuscript is due in twenty-four days (not that I'm counting). You'll never believe what I just found: *twelve* ladybugs. Yes, twelve. I counted. Twice. Did God seriously just move a tiny army of ladybugs into my workspace, right on time, to guard my final few weeks of writing? They are everywhere, but mostly perched along the door, like soldiers protecting Buckingham Palace.

Unlike other occasions when bugs have invaded my workspace, I do not reach for the vacuum. I simply stare in awe. I count them again. I laugh. Then I promptly burst into tears at the overwhelming mercy of this moment, the reminder that I am loved, known, fought for, and protected by a God who would do anything for me. A God who would send a troop of ladybugs for this last stretch of writing—our own little private signal—just when I need a pick-me-up, a smile, a bit of reassurance that I'm not alone.

Author and speaker Carey Wallace writes in *Comment* magazine, "An artist's failure to work is rarely mechanical—fingers that fail to curl around a pen or a brush—but spiritual: a fear that has rendered them artistically blind or deaf. The solution to them all is to draw closer to God, the source of all order, rest, and freedom, and of every image, sound, and word."[3]

Tonight, surrounded by ladybugs, I draw closer to my Maker as I attempt to make art that reflects Him. I light a candle and ask God to meet me on this page, believing He is the source of both my inspiration and protection. I remember the beginning of Psalm 144:

> Blessed be the LORD, my rock,
>   who trains my hands for war,
>   and my fingers for battle.

I place my fingers on the keys, and begin to write.

CREATIVE EXERCISE

Find one or more passages of Scripture to use as you fight despair, anxiety, or other forms of darkness as a mother and artist. Write them on index cards and commit them to memory.

JOURNALING PROMPT

Write a prayer for your motherhood, and a prayer for your creative work.

15

THROWING GLITTER

An hour before I push my baby girl into the world, the room is so calm and so quiet, I am almost in disbelief that a birth is about to occur. My last labor, a surprise unmedicated VBAC, produced sounds you'd expect from a horror film. This labor, on the other hand, is giving off library vibes.

I cannot stop raving about the epidural. "Seriously—you can put my face on the billboards!" I tell the nurses and doctor. *Ashlee Gadd: Epidural Ambassador for Life.*

My doctor, somewhat amused at my comments, shrugs her shoulders and says matter-of-factly, "There's no trophy for doing this without medicine."

I know this, of course. I gave birth to my second baby without medicine, and nobody handed me a trophy afterward.

Still, anytime I mention my birth stories, there's a trend among people's reactions. The scheduled C-section never raises an eyebrow, but once the phrase "drug-free VBAC" leaves my lips, eyes widen in newfound respect as if I'd just nonchalantly mentioned I'd climbed Mount Everest.

I am always quick to clarify that my second birth was less than ideal, and, if I'm honest, a bit traumatizing.

"Still—" they persist with a twinkle in their eye— "aren't you *so glad* you can say you did it?"

I never know how to answer this question. But here's a confession— those people looking at me in awe after I admit to the drug-free birth? *I used to be one of them.*

Once upon a time, I considered a drug-free birth superior to the alternative. I never said this out loud, of course, but before I had kids, I put natural birth on a secret pedestal, right up there with moms who made their own organic baby food and breastfed for twelve months. If there was a trophy reserved for birth, I believed doing it *au naturel* would earn you the biggest one.

Almost a decade into motherhood, you'd think I would know by now: *there are no trophies in this work.* Yet I still find myself silently assigning them all the time. I give a mental trophy to the mom who does daily devotions with her kids over breakfast. The mom whose house is always clean. The mom who makes healthy homemade meals (with *vegetables*! that her children *eat*!). The mom who faithfully serves the PTA, and never shows up to soccer practice without organic orange slices packed in compost-friendly packaging.

My struggle with comparison goes all the way back to childhood, to coveting my best friend's Barbie collection, which far surpassed mine. As a little girl, I compared her bedroom to my bedroom, her clothes to my clothes, her Kaboodle to my Kaboodle.

When I retired from Barbie play and entered junior high, I started comparing even more things to even more girls. I compared my grades to their grades. My hair to their hair. My A-cup bra to their C-cup bras. On to high school, college, here we go again. I compared everything from relationships and internships to career plans and dinner parties.

Now I'm a grown-up, married with three kids. I should be too old for this game, but here I am, still. Fighting the temptation to compare my home to her home. My writing to her writing. My body, my marriage, my mothering, my everything.

I know these invisible trophies aren't real.

So why do I keep comparing her nonexistent trophy collection to mine?

EVERETT AND CARSON are three grades apart. After school, they meet up on campus when the bell rings and walk together to the back gate, where I pick them up. By the time they reach the car, they've already swapped highlights from their day.

Once they're buckled in and we're exiting the pick-up line, I ask, "How was your day?"

More often than not, Carson will respond, "Bad."

When I follow up and ask him why his day was bad, he tells me about something good that happened to Everett.

Everett got a cupcake today.

Everett got to watch a movie today.

Everett got extra recess today.

When I press in, ask more questions—but why was *your* day bad?—Carson has no tangible reason, and no further explanation. His day was simply bad by comparison. His day was simply bad because something good happened to his brother.

In Matthew 20, Jesus tells a parable about laborers in the vineyard. As the story goes, the master of the house goes out into the marketplace looking for workers. He finds a group of laborers first thing in the morning, and they agree to work all day for one denarius, the equivalent of a day's wages. A few hours later, the master goes back to the marketplace for more help. Again and again, he recruits more workers throughout the day. By evening, the first laborers have worked a full, exhausting, twelve-hour shift. Meanwhile, the last laborers have only worked about an hour.

When it's time to pay the laborers and release them for the day, the master tells the foreman to pay the *last* laborers first, and to pay them one denarius as well, even though they didn't work a full day.

The first laborers, watching this exchange unfold, start to get excited. They assume they'll be paid a lot more, which makes sense, right? If you and I are doing the same job, but I work one hour and you work eight hours, you'd expect to be paid more than me.

But that's not what happens. The master gives everyone the same amount. Understandably, the first laborers are disgruntled. *Wait, what? How is that fair?*

The first laborers had no qualms about their promised wages in the beginning. They willingly agreed to one denarius as a perfectly acceptable rate. The first laborers did not become disgruntled until they witnessed someone else receiving the same amount of money for less labor. They did not become upset until they examined their work and their wages—*compared to someone else.*

Ultimately, the parable of the laborers in the vineyard is a story about a generous God who will go into the marketplace Himself, up until the final hour, heaping lavish grace on those who do not deserve it and have not earned it. This story reminds us that God abides by an upside-down kingdom, one in which the last are first and the first are last.

So the question becomes: are we going to embody the gratitude of the last laborers, or the entitlement of the first?

My pastor phrased it this way: "Are you willing to give up the idea that if you *give*, you will *get*?"[1]

If I write for seven years, surely, I'll get a book deal.

If I put my music online, surely, someone will notice me.

If I pour my heart into this creative endeavor, surely, I'll become successful.

How quickly do we forget the only trophy at stake in Kingdom-building is one of participation? Too often we default to glancing around, straining our necks, comparing our opportunities to those of the woman next to us. We start measuring our work against hers, wondering why she got a bigger toolbox, prettier material, and a better assignment than we did. We sulk in despair. We huff and puff. We sit down on the floor in protest.

We begin to question whether God, in all His infinite wisdom, actually knows what He's doing. We're back in the garden of Eden, listening to a crafty serpent try to convince us that God is not good, that He doesn't want good for us.

But we can't build the Kingdom if we don't trust the blueprints.

And we can't trust the blueprints if we don't have faith in the Architect.

SOCIAL MEDIA DID NOT EXIST when I was in high school, a fact I've silently thanked the Lord for no less than fifty times (along with the mercy of getting married before Pinterest). By the time I became a mother, I had Instagram, but the app was simpler back then. *Influencing* was not a word found in the dictionary or a degree you could pursue in college. There were no algorithms to speak of, no videos, no flashy ads. Instagram was nothing more than a chronological feed of ordinary people posting ordinary photos: babies and dogs, salads and shoes, all enhanced with the Valencia filter.

These days, social media undoubtedly makes it easier to assume everyone else is happier than us. We are bombarded daily with unrealistic standards of perfection via magazine-quality photos paired with inspiring captions. We are exposed to other people's perfectly packaged lives, broken down into bite-size squares we can scroll past while nursing our babies in the middle of the night, wearing yesterday's coffee-stained sweatpants. Just like my seven-year-old at the end of a school day, it's practically impossible not to name our day "bad" when we hold it up against everyone else's shiny pictures.

I think most of us know by now comparison is a heart issue, even though I often try to convince myself this isn't true.

Isn't comparison an Instagram issue?

A Pinterest issue?

The gorgeous-mom-at-MOPS-who-is-good-at-literally-everything issue?

Because surely if you removed all of those things from the equation, I wouldn't struggle with comparison at all. (Right?!)

Sometimes I wish there was a simple fix for comparison, like a vitamin I could take, or a setting I could toggle on in my phone. In reality, though, keeping comparison at bay requires daily, sometimes hourly, effort. To borrow a sports term (apologies to my husband, who is certainly cringing as I begin this metaphor)—battling comparison requires intentional offense and defense.

After taking two full months off Instagram in the summer of 2020, I decided to come back only half the time, deleting Instagram from my phone every other week. I felt convicted I was spending too much time on the app, and both my writing and mental health were suffering as a result. I had taken sporadic, month-long social media sabbaticals in the past, but I wanted to normalize stepping away from Instagram on a predictable, consistent basis. I craved more margin in my schedule, more scroll-free days, more time to focus on my relationships and creative work. I wanted to create a rhythm where I could actually *enjoy* social media without feeling like it sucked the life out of me.

This one-week-on/one-week-off routine has been a real game-changer, not only for the mental health benefits and the additional time it's afforded me to pursue my creative endeavors, but also because this rhythm helps me flow between defense and offense mode.

In defense mode, I shut everything down. I delete Instagram from my phone, intentionally limiting sources that can (and do!) stir up feelings of discontentment in me. I make my whole world smaller for a while.

In offense mode, I put the app back on my phone and turn into a full-blown cheerleader. I bust out my flashy posters and confetti, screaming into a megaphone, using too many exclamation points. I compliment and encourage and applaud the women in my feeds, as often as possible, as loudly as I can.

It might sound like these strategies contradict each other, but I actually find them complementary, especially when employed regularly. I spend one week reveling in silence, followed by one week giving standing ovations. Rinse, repeat.

It's like that saying—what you feed grows; what you starve dies. When we stop scrolling, stop checking our phone every five minutes, stop compulsively counting likes and trophies, we starve comparison.

Likewise, when we make a conscious habit of cheering and extolling others, offering heaps of support and genuine encouragement, we grow hearts for community.

MY MOTHER-IN-LAW WRAPS everything in glitter wrapping paper. It's become somewhat of a joke over the years—the way we find glitter two weeks after any given holiday, shimmering on the couch cushions or wedged in the crevices of the dining room table, leftover sparkles reminding us Mimi was here.

"Elegant gaudy" is her style of choice, the polar opposite of mine. She loves bright; I love muted. She loves shiny; I love matte. We've learned this about each other over the course of almost two decades of being in each other's lives. Nowadays, when she shops for me, she tones down. When I shop for her, I scale up.

There's something else you should know about my mother-in-law: she supports my work like crazy. She will buy, I am not kidding, probably seventy-five copies of this book you're reading. She comments on every single thing I've ever written. Every time I have an idea churning in my head, she calls it brilliant and asks how she can help support me. I've started thinking of my mother-in-law as a glitter-thrower, both literally and figuratively.

Not everyone in my life is like her, though.

Have you ever known someone who seems to thrive on picking apart your ideas and dreams the minute you say them out loud?

When we stop scrolling, stop checking our phone every five minutes, stop compulsively counting likes and trophies, we starve comparison.

Julia Cameron has a perfect metaphor for this:

> We have, many of us, had the experience of being all dressed
> up, ready to go somewhere and feeling pretty marvelous, when
> someone—a parent, a friend, even the baby-sitter—picks a small
> piece of lint off our outfit. "Lint picking" is focusing on the small
> imperfection rather than seeing the greater glory of the whole.[2]

I've been creating for a very long time, and I've had a fair share of
lint picked off me. I know what it feels like to say a dream out loud and
have my words met with immediate skepticism, an eye roll, a huff, a
puff, a passive-aggressive remark. I've tossed an idea in the air like a
balloon and watched someone stab it with a pen.

But, and this is much harder to admit, I know how to be a lint
picker, too. I have, at times, looked at someone else's work and mentally shredded it like a block of cheese. I assume privately criticizing
others will somehow make me feel better about myself, but lint-
picking always disappoints.

Do you know what never disappoints? Throwing glitter.

For all the times I've battled comparison, I have never once regret-
ted being generous—with my money, my time, my likes, my shares,
my comments, my praise, my encouragement. If what we feed grows,
this is what I want to feed: my own capacity to celebrate others well. If
I live to be ninety-five years old, I hope to have a hoarse voice from a
life spent cheering too loudly for those around me. I desperately want
to leave a trail of glitter in my wake.

Throwing glitter is sometimes easier said than done. But I promise
you this: the more glitter you intentionally throw with your hands, the
more glitter you start to automatically throw with your heart.

Every day we get to choose how we show up in this world. We get to
choose whether we celebrate or mock other people's dreams. We get
to choose whether we dole out praise or intentionally withhold it. We

If I live to be ninety-five years old, I hope to have a hoarse voice from a life spent cheering too loudly for those around me.

get to choose whether we build one another up or break each other down, whether we root *for* or *against* our fellow moms, our fellow artists, our fellow Kingdom-builders.

I don't know about you, but I want to choose generosity over grumbling. Compliments over criticism. Glitter-throwing over lint-picking. Let's like and share and comment too much. Let's use an obnoxious number of emojis. Let's spur the women around us toward love and good deeds, and whatever beautiful work God has set before them.

And who knows? Two or three weeks from now, someone might find traces of glitter lingering on the couch cushions, right when they need a sparkly reminder to keep going.

CREATIVE EXERCISE

Go throw some metaphorical glitter on someone today. Take a minute to drop a fellow mom or artist a note, a DM, or an email. Pay them a genuine compliment and encourage them to keep going.

JOURNALING PROMPT

In what areas do you struggle with comparison? Be gut-wrenchingly honest. How might you work toward throwing glitter in those very places?

16

MISSION OVER METRICS

"Five pounds, four ounces!" the nurse calls out from the scale.

Our second baby, Carson, has just arrived a month early, much to everyone's surprise, including mine and Brett's. A few hours ago, we walked into the birth center without a clue, a car seat, or an adequately packed hospital bag. Apparently, that was *not* false labor.

His tiny body almost fits in my hand. We text the grandparents: *Can you pick up some preemie clothes and diapers?* Over the next few days, Carson's weight is closely monitored by doctors and nurses. By the time we are discharged, he is down to four pounds, fourteen ounces.

"A slight dip is normal," the pediatrician reassures us, "but you should continue breastfeeding as often as possible."

Always a good student, I follow directions and transform myself into a human milk machine, nursing on demand, all day, every day.

I pop fenugreek like candy, make lactation cookies every afternoon, pump after every morning feeding. Despite my best efforts, one week later at the next doctor's appointment, Carson is still not on the growth chart.

We start going back for weigh-ins every two weeks. Every time, I hold my breath while the numbers flash. I start to associate the number on the scale with my overall performance as a mother. Every time the doctor smiles at the scale, I am filled with temporary confidence. Every time the doctor frowns, I am crushed with insecurity. This becomes a pattern, a way of life, a regular math test I cannot seem to pass. Numbers live in my head 24/7: growth charts, ounces, statistics, BMI rankings. I continue to nurse on demand, pump, buy lactation pills and potions. The doctor continues to request weigh-ins, asking me the same series of questions at each appointment.

How many times a day does he nurse?

How many times a day do you pump?

How many ounces of breastmilk are you producing?

I try to keep track of all the numbers, occasionally fabricating them out of desperation to prove myself capable, a good student, a good mother. When my son starts solid foods, I mix avocado and olive oil into everything he eats. I spoon feed him guacamole and heaps of peanut butter, convinced the progression of his development is resting squarely on my shoulders, on the calorie content of every ounce of food I offer him.

None of my efforts feel like enough.

I start to associate the number on the scale with my overall performance as a mother.

Around the one-year mark, I finally work up the courage to ask the doctor point-blank: *What exactly is your biggest concern with Carson's weight?* The pediatrician stares at me, blinks a few times, and mutters something about wanting to make sure my son grows up to be taller than five feet.

I stare back at him in disbelief. *THIS is the main concern? His hypothetical future height?* I walk out of that office feeling ten pounds lighter, an overwhelming sense of relief filling my mind for the first time in a year. I also feel like an idiot. How many nights had I lost sleep over these weigh-ins? How many days had I pulled up the Internet growth charts and obsessively compared his precise dot placement to that of other babies?

How many times had I paid more attention to Carson's weight than the whole picture of who he was becoming? How many times had I measured my success as a mother by arbitrary numbers flashing on a scale?

I LAUNCH THE COFFEE + CRUMBS BLOG on an ordinary Tuesday, six months pregnant, not at all concerned about my ability to manage a new passion project while caring for a toddler and soon-to-be newborn.

Weeks later, though, my tiny dream unexpectedly becomes an overnight success. I now have my own profile on the *Huffington Post*. My inbox explodes. People want to interview me, work for me, send me free products to review. I am overwhelmed, equal parts thrilled and dizzy, trying to keep up with the new demands of what is starting to feel like a very real job I conjured up out of thin air.

Before I know it, baby number two is in my arms and the dominoes begin to fall. I'm holding a baby I think is too small and a job I fear is too big. I am bombarded with so many emails, so many opportunities, so many questions from so many people. I say *yes* and *sure* and *of course* without fully processing what I am doing, what I am committing to, how these obligations are going to affect my heart, my family, my life. To outsiders looking in, I appear to be thriving, climbing the rungs on the ladder to success, well on my way to the peak of a self-made career. On the inside, though, I feel nothing short of panicked. Coffee + Crumbs is becoming too big, too fast, above and beyond what I had initially envisioned. *Is this even what I want? This much ongoing responsibility? This much pressure?*

I am fearful of the fast-growing numbers, the rapid exposure, the overwhelming amount of praise and criticism I am suddenly receiving through a fire hose. I am secretly terrified of lurking Internet trolls, worried we're going to become one of those websites people hate for sport.

But most of all, I am scared that Coffee + Crumbs is turning into a machine I never wanted it to be, that I'm going to wake up one day and forget the heart of why I started all of this in the first place.

SARAH PEREZ

METAL ARTIST
SACRAMENTO, CALIFORNIA
@ELECTRICSUNCREATIVES

Q: If you could give moms who long to create as they raise their children a word of advice or encouragement, what would it be?

A: Please do it. We need you fully alive and tapping into your voice. The world needs you to bring forth beauty and honesty into the world—something from your own head and hands. Whether another human will see or experience it beyond your walls makes little difference. Being a part of the creative process has the potential to produce the fruit of vulnerability, tenderness, openness, and curiosity, not to mention pure delight and joy. I think we need more of that rippling out from our homes into our communities and world: creative moms open to themselves, open to God, open to others—tender and alive to the beauty of life. Expressing our creativity can do that.

OVER THE YEARS, I've attended conferences and listened to experts preach the importance of growth, growth, growth. I see it every day in my social media ads: *Click Here to Learn How I Grew My Email List from 500 to 50,000 in One Month!* Since launching Coffee + Crumbs, numerous people—well-meaning friends included—have encouraged me at times to pursue more website traffic, more podcast downloads, more Instagram followers, more money.

And I have been tempted, more than once, to take their advice. To put their steps into place, to try XYZ, to move forward with a plan for *More*＿＿＿＿＿ as the end goal. I've dabbled in their ideas, tried their strategies on like hats. But in the end, those methods left me feeling empty, even when they worked. Because in the midst of a culture pressuring me to put my worth in the number of Instagram followers at the top of my profile, or dollars in my bank account, I have felt the still, small voice of God calling me back to this question: *Whose measuring stick are you using, anyway?*

After some of our initial Coffee + Crumbs content went viral, I started measuring everything we did against those numbers. If an essay didn't get 500-plus shares on Facebook, I felt disappointed and insecure. Little did I know, Facebook was in the process of overhauling their algorithms altogether, and we would never see numbers like that again. Not even close.

I had been working with an unreliable, ever-changing measuring stick.

Thankfully, God began nudging me toward a more stable barometer, one in which numbers and statistics do not define who I am, or the value of my work. This shift did not happen overnight. But gradually, with time, I noticed my own reactions beginning to soften. I wasn't so quick to despair when an essay performed badly, just like I wasn't so quick to jump up and down when an essay performed well. I started putting less emphasis on the number of likes and shares, and more weight in a single comment that said, "I needed these words today." I started to embrace the idea that the art I put into the world matters, and contains worth, regardless of what the analytics say.

At the end of my life, God isn't looking for a blue check mark on my Instagram profile. He is looking for my faithfulness.

And I'm learning faithfulness doesn't always look like the world's version of success. It doesn't always result in the biggest applause. Sometimes faithfulness looks like taking your podcast out of iTunes at the height of its success. Sometimes faithfulness looks like going dark on social media for two full months when the experts call that

At the end of my life, God isn't looking for a blue check mark on my Instagram profile. He is looking for my faithfulness.

algorithm suicide. Sometimes faithfulness looks like saying no to advertising dollars and sponsorship campaigns you feel would jeopardize the integrity of your work. Sometimes faithfulness looks like choosing less over more, simple over grand, humble rhythms over impressive stats.

Faithfulness looks like listening, like planting your feet in quiet obedience where God has called you. Faithfulness looks like committing to mission over metrics.

There's nothing inherently wrong with wanting to build our platforms or be compensated for our art. But there is a difference between stewarding our work well and chasing numbers for the sake of chasing numbers. Because when we start thinking of actual, real human beings solely in terms of "followers"—we miss out on the opportunity to love and serve them well. When an obsession with growth takes up more space in our hearts than the God we want to glorify, we miss the whole point. When we focus more on the worldly outcome of our efforts than the inner rewards of using our God-given gifts, we've put our treasure in the wrong place.

I wish I could tell you I've overcome this tension, that numbers have lost all meaning to me. The truth is, I still sometimes struggle to put my faith in what's unseen over the number of followers and likes flashing in my face each day. Likewise, I sometimes struggle to remember my "success" as a mother has nothing to do with my children's weight, or their report cards, or the number of hours I have or haven't allowed them to sit in front of a screen.

I sometimes forget the posture of my heart cannot be logged in a chart.

Here's the thing about numbers: they go up and down. They always have and they always will. Your baby can sleep six hours one night, and three hours the next. Your podcast downloads can go up the same month your book sales go down. You can be on top one day, and on the bottom the next. The world is finicky like that, built on circumstances and algorithms that are always changing.

But when we choose mission over metrics, we put our faith, our work, our love in a God who never changes. When we choose mission over metrics, we put our motherhood and creativity in the hands of Someone not contained by math.

Your podcast may not ever land in the top one hundred shows. Your child may not ever get past the fifth percentile on the growth chart. You might show up for a speaking event one day and find far more empty chairs than attendees (ask me how I know). You might not ever look like the world's picture of a successful mom or a successful artist.

But that doesn't mean God isn't working through you and in you, for a good and glorious purpose. You can fall short of the world's standards for success while simultaneously reaping a Kingdom harvest. One holds you captive; one sets you free.

We can take heart in a God who is capable of using every ounce of our mothering, and every ounce of our art, for sacred work that can never be measured in numbers.

CREATIVE EXERCISE

Write a mission statement for your creative work, or the *why* behind your creativity.

JOURNALING PROMPT

Write about a time you got swept up in numbers, either in your mothering or creativity. Looking back, how could a "mission over metrics" mindset have helped you?

17

REST

Hours after Carson was born, I insisted Brett go home, retrieve my laptop, and bring it back to the birth center. What I wouldn't give to go back in time and gently grasp that version of myself by the shoulders—lying in a hospital bed after a traumatic birth, bleeding, responding to emails as if my life depended on it—and whisper: *Sweetheart, you don't have to live this way.*

I did not take a maternity leave. At the time, I would have told you I didn't have a choice. Today, I'd tell you I had a choice, and I chose wrong.

Four days postpartum, I planted my toddler in front of *Sesame Street* and created an office in my bed next to my five-pound baby. Coffee + Crumbs was three months old and growing rapidly. I started working more and more and more, a looming fear of failure hovering over me at all times. As a number of potential endeavors arrived in my inbox, I felt a mounting pressure to keep up, to steward every single opportunity with care, not just for myself, but for every woman on my team.

As my workload increased, my childcare did not. My almost full-time job paid a fraction of a part-time job. I could not afford more help, so I stayed up late and woke up early instead, even though I was up with a crying baby every night.

Sleep-deprived and bone-tired, I pushed through the days like an athlete at training camp. With a baby strapped to my chest and a toddler running circles around me, I worked in my bed, on the couch, at the dining room table, fueled by multiple cups of lukewarm coffee. My laptop and phone were never out of reach. I brought work to the park, to the carwash, to the doctor's office. I squeezed productivity out of every last second of the day, the way you squeeze out the last molecule of toothpaste.

And isn't that the ultimate mother's dream? To be able to stay at home with her kids and work from anywhere? Anytime?

Let me clarify: I worked *everywhere*. I worked *all the time*.

During the day, I wore my exhaustion like a badge of honor. In the stillness of the night, though, I started to feel like the world's biggest hypocrite for running an online community for mothers while ignoring my own children to do it.

THE FIRST TIME I ATTEMPT SABBATH, an intentional day of rest and worship, I don't know what to do with my hands. I am like a toddler who cannot sit still for story time at the library. Fidgety. Twitchy. My hands are desperate for something to do—a keyboard to type on, dishes to wash, a vacuum to hold. I feel out of my element, profoundly uncomfortable being still.

I'm determined to try, though, because I've just finished reading *Rhythms of Rest* by Shelly Miller, a book that may have changed my life. When I get to the last page, I am compelled to call an emergency meeting with Brett.

"We need to start practicing Sabbath. *Immediately*," I tell him.

For what it's worth, I memorized the ten commandments by the time I was five or six years old. I grew up attending church three times a week, including a rigorous hour-long "Bible Lab"—which I'd now describe as Sunday school on steroids. As a young girl, I tucked most of the commandments easily into my heart: do not lie, do not steal, do not covet. *Got it, Lord. Will try my best.*

But one commandment seemed easy to ignore (and I did, for thirty-five years): the one about keeping the Sabbath holy. I don't know why, but I always filed Sabbath under "optional"—as if it were an extra credit opportunity instead of a real assignment.

I've embraced Sabbath moments, sure. I know how to get lost in a riveting book for an hour in the backyard. I know how to power nap, how to put my feet up for fifteen minutes at the end of a long day. But ceasing work for twenty-four hours? Regularly? Giving up one whole day a week in the name of rest? That's always seemed . . . excessive. Unnecessary. Dare I say *impossible*?

I've been a hard worker for as long as I can remember. I learned early on—in my home, school, and church—that fewer things in life carried more value than a strong work ethic. It's one of the first rhythms I remember learning as a child: work hard, accomplish goals, receive praise. Rinse, repeat.

As I met goal after goal—obtaining good grades, landing a role in the school play, making the cheerleading squad—I learned to associate

I started to feel like the world's biggest hypocrite for running an online community for mothers while ignoring my own children to do it.

"working hard" with "receiving praise." And I *liked* receiving praise. I liked knowing my parents and teachers were proud of me. So I carried this strategy into my adult life, straight into my career. I became known as the girl who always went the extra mile. I did whatever my bosses asked of me and then some, happily offering to stay late, often creating my own extra credit assignments.

I spent most of my twenties running the proverbial rat race. The harder I worked, the more praise I received. All of the *good jobs* and *I'm so proud of yous* hit my body like endorphins.

When I started Coffee + Crumbs, people *ooohed* and *aaahed*—more praise, more praise, more praise. Every positive remark felt like a dose of worth and self-esteem being pumped through an IV straight into my veins. And like a little child, I beamed. I felt approved. Accepted. Loved.

I couldn't get enough of that feeling, so I worked harder and harder and harder.

AFTER RUNNING COFFEE + CRUMBS for almost four years, I hit a breaking point. Within the span of just a few months, my workload tripled, Brett and I moved our family into a fixer-upper, and I got pregnant with our third baby.

Our house became a construction zone filled with dust, incessant pounding, and dozens of cardboard boxes that still needed to be unpacked. Consumed by nausea, I spent most days on the verge of puking. Meanwhile, my work with Coffee + Crumbs had never been busier. We took our podcast from biweekly to weekly, hosted our first virtual event, and launched an online membership community for creative moms, all at the same time.

Somewhere between the stress of my job, the costly issues with our new (very, very old) house, and the general anxiety of what turned into a highly monitored pregnancy after my second baby was born prematurely, I stopped sleeping. Every night, I'd lie awake making to-do lists in my head, hyper aware of every failure, every unanswered email, every little thing slipping through the cracks. I criticized myself constantly, keeping a steady record of every misstep, every person I had disappointed. My heart raced every time I opened my laptop. I cried easily. I stopped exercising, stopped reading, stopped taking care of myself physically and mentally. My pregnant body ached all the time, barely sustained by cereal and takeout. I couldn't seem to make time for anything. Clipping my own fingernails felt like an unnecessary indulgence.

I did not have the language for it at the time, but I know now I was practically sprinting toward burnout. My husband could see it. My team members could see it. Everyone could see I was drowning but me. I do not recall who initially made the suggestion, but someone, at some point, asked, "Ashlee, do you need to take a break?"

A *break*?

I remember scoffing at what seemed like an impossible suggestion at the time.

For so long, I had clung to the belief that I was the glue holding everything and everyone together. It wasn't until I became a shell of myself—crying all the time, lashing out at my family, suffering from chronic insomnia—that I could finally admit, *I can't keep living this way.* My job had become my entire life. It wasn't until God met me at my breaking point and gently began unclenching my fists—loosening the tight grasp I had on my to-do list, my productivity, and my highly valued work ethic—that I could finally see the damage my own ego, pride, and inflated sense of self-importance had caused.

Eventually, between my own desperate prayers for guidance and the consistent encouragement of my friends and family, I surrendered. Everyone was right. I needed a break. My obsession with my job had become toxic, unhealthy, and unsustainable. I emailed the Coffee +

Crumbs team: *We're taking a sabbatical in August. No essays, no podcasts, no newsletter.*

Do you know what happened when I put the "out of office" message on all four of my inboxes? Do you know what happened when Coffee + Crumbs went dark on social media for a whole month, and we did not produce a single thing for thirty days?

Nothing.

FOR YEARS, I have bought into the lie that I am what I do, that I am only as valuable and worthy as my last accomplishment. My identity and my creative work have often felt one and the same, twisted around each other like a soft pretzel with no beginning and no end. I have often operated from a deep-seated belief that if I stop working, stop producing, stop performing—nobody will love me anymore.

This I-am-what-I-do mentality is why I filed "Sabbath" under "optional." This is why I didn't take any kind of maternity leave after Carson was born. This is why I scoffed at the idea of a sabbatical. All along, I had convinced myself that I was the key ingredient in every recipe, and if I were to clock out, for any amount of time, my whole world would shatter as a result.

Only in recent years have I come to see this line of thinking for what it really is: a "confession of unbelief" as Jen Wilkin writes in *Ten Words to Live By*. In her chapter on keeping the Sabbath holy, Wilkins equates an unwillingness to rest with "an admission that we view ourselves as creator and sustainer of our own universe."[1]

Rest helps us remember that God is God, and we're not God. Rest forces us to accept our own limitations and put our faith in the One who intentionally designed us to need Him. With this foundation, we can stop viewing rest as a sign of weakness or laziness, and instead start viewing rest as a sign of faith, trust, and glorious surrender.

Our culture loves to paint rest as a self-care issue, but rest is—and has always been—a *faith* issue.

Bubble baths and pedicures are great, but do you know what's even better? Realizing there is nothing we could ever do to earn the love and grace and rest that has already been given to us. We can labor all day and all night, we can hustle and strive and bulldoze to accomplish more and more and more, but at the end of the day, none of those efforts would even begin to make a dent in what's already been done at the cross.

Dearest reader, *you are not what you do.* You are not the art you make. You are not the number of followers displayed at the top of your Instagram profile. You are not the framed awards hanging on your wall or the praise on other people's lips. You are a beloved daughter of the Highest King, who gave His life so you could *live.* So you could *rest.* So you could be free from the desperate pursuit of trying to earn your keep in this world.

Unlike us, God doesn't grow tired or weary. He doesn't need rest like we do. But after God created, He rested anyway—giving us a blueprint, a rhythm, an order. There is a time to work, a time to create, a time to show up and put your butt in the chair, but there is also a time to let your body, mind, and soul hit the pause button.

Nine weeks before this manuscript was due, I had a miscarriage. At the time, I held myself to a rigorous writing schedule: I wrote every morning from five thirty to seven thirty, every Tuesday and Thursday night from five to eight, and every Saturday from nine in the morning to one in the afternoon.

The day I learned my fourth pregnancy was not viable, I came home, crawled into bed, and barely got out of it for two weeks. I watched sixty-three episodes of *Friday Night Lights* in the span of twelve days. That's 2,835 minutes I spent watching TV during a time I had already deemed "crunch mode."

And even though I knew my body and mind needed rest, even though I was bleeding and couldn't stop crying, a tiny voice in the back of my head still chanted: *deadline, deadline, deadline.*

I had to remind myself, again, that rest is an act of faith.

I had to go back to the basics, back to the foundation, back to obedience and trust. *Do I believe God wants me to write this book?* Yes. *Do I believe God is going to provide me the time I need to finish it?* (Quieter) Yes. *Do I believe I can rest for two weeks after having a miscarriage, and still finish this book on time?* (Long pause) Yes.

IN THE FALL OF 2020, Brett and I booked a relaxing weekend away to celebrate his birthday. We had been looking forward to the trip for weeks, anticipating a much-needed break from our jobs, children, and the never-ending news cycle. Twenty-four hours before check-in, though, our plans fell apart with a single unmet deadline. Brett was in charge of a critical project at work, and it wasn't done yet.

"I can't leave," he said as he cringed. "I'm so sorry. You should go by yourself."

We had already paid for the trip, but the only way I could justify an unexpected weekend alone in a hotel room would be to work the whole time. A to-do list started forming in my head. I began to panic out loud, already feeling behind, unprepared, stressed, and overwhelmed at the thought of staring at a computer screen for forty-eight hours, when that wasn't the original plan for the weekend.

After listening to me unravel for several minutes, Brett proposed, "So why don't you just . . . *rest*? Read books, sleep, watch movies, order takeout?"

The idea was preposterous. No matter what he said, my default worker bee mindset could not wrap my head around the idea of a weekend away in a fancy hotel, all by myself, with no agenda, for no reason. Surely I'd need to write, or clean out all my inboxes, or make progress on my own work deadlines to justify the expense of the hotel and the fact that my mother-in-law would be watching our kids.

"Let's just get a refund," I said.

He insisted: *Please, please go.* He already felt bad enough.

"This feels too extravagant," I argued back. "I don't deserve it."

I checked in with friends and asked for advice. Every single one of them encouraged me to go. My friend Sarah reframed the offer: "You're right, this *is* extravagant. But our God is a generous God. So go. And enjoy the weekend."

Tears stung my eyes as my friend reminded me that when we embrace rest, we are not only placing our faith in God's provision over the work of our hands, we are also receiving a *gift.* And an extravagant one, at that.

I filled an overnight bag with pajamas and face masks, popcorn and books. I spent two nights in a hotel room reading, journaling, and watching movies. During the day, I wandered the streets, popping in

> The quieter I get, the more I hear God's still, small voice, reminding me rest is a gift, not a burden. A mercy, not a sacrifice.

and out of little boutiques and bookstores. I bought myself fresh eucalyptus at a tiny flower stand. I ate pasta in a fluffy robe on crisp white sheets. I took a hike through the forest, filling my camera roll with dozens of pictures of sunlight streaming through the redwood trees.

That weekend, I became so quiet and so still, I could hear my own heart beating. The time away felt like love, like grace, like a gift I didn't deserve—wholly and unequivocally extravagant.

Six months later, when I felt convicted to start practicing Sabbath (and roped my family into joining me!), the day did not feel like a gift at first. I struggled to leave dishes in the sink, crumbs on the floor, emails unread and unanswered. Setting aside work and chores, for one whole day a week, felt more like a sacrifice, like something I was giving up. And in a sense, I was. I was giving up a day of productivity, not to mention the delicious feeling of accomplishment I experience after a hard day's work.

Week after week, though, God met me in my pride and self-reliance. He gently turned my inner monologue upside down: Forget what *you're* giving *me*—look what *I'm* giving *you*. Unrushed time with your children. A break from staring at a screen. Board games. Nature. Quiet. Time to read. Time to worship. Time to pause.

Slowly but surely, little by little, I am learning to quiet the hustling part of my brain, the voice that wants me to believe I am only loved for what I do. The quieter I get, the more I hear God's still, small voice, reminding me rest is a gift, not a burden. A mercy, not a sacrifice.

Rest reminds us how beloved we are, just as we are, with nothing to prove and nothing to earn.

CREATIVE EXERCISE

Consider what activities are restful to you, what lights you up, what sorts of things you can do for hours with a smile on your face. Reading? Wandering around the farmer's market? Going on a walk with a podcast in your earbuds? This week, plan a time of rest. Surrender your to-do list, and take note of how you feel afterward.

JOURNALING PROMPT

What would rest as an act of faith look like for you, in this season?

18

OPEN HANDS

Presley had just taken her first wobbly steps when a global pandemic flipped the world upside down. Like a tiny queen locked in a nineteen-hundred-square-foot castle, she spent most of her second year of life practically under house arrest. She learned to walk by toddling across the same vinyl floors and the same patch of lawn, day after day after day. The zoo closed. The library closed. Even the playgrounds near our house remained wrapped in caution tape for the better part of 2020.

Miraculously, from what I could tell, Presley didn't seem to notice our lifestyle change. Every morning she wandered into the kitchen to empty her favorite drawer, again, as if it were full of fresh treasure and not the same set of Tupperware she emptied yesterday. After that, she'd happily pluck Honey Nut Cheerios out of the same plastic bowl, carefully dropping them into the same toy teacups, grinning ear to ear as if she'd never accomplished a greater feat.

Presley was the only member of our family who never seemed to mind the perpetual Groundhog Day, finding just as much joy and contentment in the identical batch of activities she had completed the day before.

The first few times we took her out of the house that year, she only wanted to *run*—as if she were tasting freedom for the very first time, desperate to gulp it down. We ventured to an open field one night for family photos, and she ran away from us the entire time, laughing hysterically like it was the best day of her life. She soaked up every ounce of her liberation that evening, the glory of being outside with no fence and no boundaries, hair blowing in the wind.

On Presley's second birthday, I couldn't help but grieve all that was taken from her the previous year. I thought of little, insignificant things: the simple joy of riding in a shopping cart, attending story time at the library, having playdates with friends her own age—all things I did with my boys at that age. I took an ounce of comfort in knowing she had no clue what she had missed, and that, to her, every day at home with her toys and her brothers and a faded trampoline might as well have been Disneyland.

But as I watched my daughter blow out the two candles on her cake, another lament crossed my mind. While Presley spent almost a whole year missing out on everything the world had to offer, the world also missed out on *her*—her smile, her laugh, the way she calls Cheerios "cheeries." This girl is a bottle of pure sunshine, portable joy. On the very worst days of a dark, dreary, terrifying year, she still enchanted us. How would we have survived the turmoil and uncertainty of the pandemic without her antics, her giggles, the innocent sound of her tiny feet running down the hall keeping us afloat?

My daughter's sheer existence was a gift, a life raft of sorts, one I desperately wanted to share with others in a year filled with chaos.

I NEVER THOUGHT I'd grow up to be an overprotective mom. You know, the ones who hover like buzzing bees, obsessing over germs and potential dangers and those little fabric shopping cart covers?

That is . . . until I had my own baby.

Because once I had my own baby, I didn't want anything or anyone to touch him. (I ended up registering for the blue polka dot shopping cart cover, for what it's worth.) *Overprotective* would be an understatement. I became a full-blown momma bear, and fast. Anytime we'd leave the house, as soon as we got out of the car, I'd immediately place Everett in one of those forty-yards-of-fabric baby wraps to ensure nobody could take him from me. I tied him to my chest like a baby prisoner.

On the rare occasion I'd relinquish him into the arms of someone else, I'd stand exactly two feet away, lurking with crazy eyes like a jealous ex-girlfriend. I'd use breastfeeding as an excuse to get him back, even if it wasn't time to feed him yet. Looking back, I think hoarding my own baby was somewhat typical first-time mom behavior. But I can also now freely admit—some of my overprotectiveness was selfish. Anyone who has ever held a baby knows about the intoxicating newborn scent, the way your heart swells when they flash you a gummy grin, the oxytocin release from simple skin-to-skin contact.

As a new mom, I didn't care about sharing all of that goodness with others.

I wanted to keep my baby all to myself.

I RECENTLY READ a newsletter by writer Courtney Martin titled "I Love. . ."—a compilation of sentences that all began the same way.

> I love rye toast at diners. I love finishing a book. I love Ruffles, cottage cheese, and The Oprah Winfrey Show circa 1996. I love how insignificant Redwoods make me feel. I love asking questions. I love the river, how it obliterates time.[1]

At the top of her post, she gave credit to the original source of inspiration, a poem by Alex Dimitrov.[2] By the time I got to the bottom of Courtney's list, I could not wait to write my own. The more I wrote, the more ideas I had.

I started my list on a Wednesday afternoon, and I woke up at three the next morning with a dozen more lines swirling in my head. Every sentence bred another sentence. I got out of bed at four, started a pot of coffee, and curled up on the couch with my laptop. I couldn't believe how many things I loved.

I love the smell of the first rain. I love peanut butter and bananas on my waffles. I love dinner parties. I love (tasteful) bathroom graffiti. I love when I happen to see something awkward at the same time as a stranger, and we lock eyes for a moment, like, "Yeah, I saw that, too."

I LOVE

I love to eavesdrop on airplanes. I love getting a great parking spot on the first try. I love a high maintenance skincare routine. I love a low maintenance personality. I love Diet Dr Pepper. I love day-two hair. I love when a song comes on the radio that you haven't heard in ten years, but you still know every single word. I love making friends on the Internet. I love a good recommendation. I love freckles. I love nostalgia. I love cliffhangers. I love to follow sunlight around the house like a cat. I love the way squirrels eat fruit with their hands like humans. I love a cotton candy sky. I love when you trim a plant down to the roots and it grows back bigger and better than before. I love a good metaphor. I love when applause spurs an encore. I love old people holding hands. I love the feeling of freshly shaved legs (mine) and a freshly shaved face (his). I love lighting candles for no reason. I love inside jokes. I love smack talk during board games. I love the beach, how endless everything feels—the sand, the water, the sky, God's grace. I love friends who forgive. I love second chances. I love when Brett throws something at me and I catch it, and he falls in love with me all over again. I love how I look in heels. I love how I feel in slippers. I love finding the

Halfway through composing my list, I roped my mastermind group into joining me. All four of us published our lists on the same day, on our personal blogs, and we each posted a snippet to Instagram as well.

Comments poured in quickly on all of our posts. *I love this! I want to make a list!* By the end of the day, more than forty people had written their own versions. In the following weeks, more and more people participated in the prompt, not because they had been explicitly invited to, but because they were simply inspired reading the other lists circulating around and couldn't help but write their own.

Just like that, the "I love" prompt spread like wildfire—first from Alex Dimitrov to Courtney Martin, then to me, to my mastermind group, then to dozens, and eventually hundreds of people on Instagram.

Creativity is, and will always be, generative.

perfect gift. I love when my inbox is less than ten. I love to learn. I love permission to change my mind. I love waking up before anyone else. I love getting rid of toys. I love a good charcuterie board. I love being in the company of women who unabashedly champion each other. I love pep talks. I love sleeping with the windows open. I love that I can't stop thinking about how many things I love. I love(d) writing this.

YOUR TURN

Make a list of things you love.
If you'd like, use #theiloveprompt
on Instagram.

When someone shares their art with the world, that masterpiece, whatever it may be, has the power to inspire someone else to create. Another person creates and shares, which then inspires someone else to create and share, and so on and so forth. Creativity has an endless ripple effect.

In the past year, I've read three thought-provoking books by authors who are no longer alive. From convicting me to start practicing Sabbath to simply inspiring me to write, each book impacted me for different reasons.

In a world where we often consume content on the Internet in thirty-second spurts, I rarely think about the long-lasting effects of my creative work. I certainly never think about my work outliving me. More often than not, I assume my art has a shelf life of twenty-four hours before it disappears into the black hole of cyberspace.

At the same time, I can easily recall art that has left a mark on me—books, essays, poems, photographs, music—creative work that has shaped me, moved me, influenced the way I think, the way I write, the way I approach my craft as a whole. I am abundantly thankful to the artists who, as Jean Rhys says, "feed the lake."[3] Part of the reason I am still creating today is because of the inspiring work other artists have generously poured into the world before me.

When I start to think of my creative work as a living, breathing thing, I am propelled forward to create not only with a sense of urgency, but also with a generous heart, one that is willing to give more of my art away.

Because isn't it an honor, a miracle even, to play a teeny tiny role in this creative ecosystem? Doesn't it leave you a little awestruck to know

Part of the reason I am still creating today is because of the inspiring work other artists have generously poured into the world before me.

the art we create today could potentially inspire and impact generations to come?

WE HAD JUST PULLED THE CAR into the garage when Brett noticed a bunch of missed calls on his phone. We both knew something was wrong. Brett got out of the car and quickly called his brother, standing in the driveway.

I will never forget the sight of his legs buckling, hearing him say over and over again with a desperate voice, "Don't say that. Don't say that."

Without hearing anything else, I knew. I retrieved Everett from his car seat and carried him to where Brett stood, crying, his head in his hands. I gently touched Brett's shoulder, not wanting to startle him.

"My dad just died," he said, choking back sobs. I began crying myself, sandwiching Everett between our bodies in a hug. I didn't know what to say. I didn't know what else to do.

Minutes later, we haphazardly threw clothes in a duffel bag and got back in the car. I followed Brett's lead on the drive, letting him talk when he wanted to, but leaving ample space in the air for silence, for tears, for sorrow. I never let go of his hand.

Ninety minutes later, we pulled up to the house where his dad had taken his final breath.

Brett got out of the car slowly. I followed him up the walkway, carrying Everett, tenderly crossing the threshold into the house. We all congregated near the front door, whispering condolences to one another. Grief hung in the air like fog.

I locked eyes with my mother-in-law, her face splotchy with tears. I felt the weight of death hovering over us, all while holding fifteen pounds of fresh life on my hip. Without saying a word, I reached out and placed Everett—the baby I wanted no one but me to hold—in her arms. He was the only gift I could think to offer.

A FEW WEEKS AFTER MY MISCARRIAGE, I opened a package in the mail from my friend and pen pal, Melissa. Inside was a ladybug card, alongside a "Monk Mode" mix CD to play while I write, and a folded piece of paper containing a poem.

She wrote, "The poem I'm sending you came to me in the middle of the night after losing my first pregnancy. It was a real gift from God, as I rarely experience writing that way—where the whole thing just downloads."

I read Melissa's poem sitting at my kitchen table with tears streaming down my face.

The day of my D&C, I recalled three essays about miscarriage. One, by my friend April, had mentioned the comfort of warm socks. I was told not to bring anything to the surgery center but my phone and ID, but I smuggled in a pair of fuzzy socks anyway, thinking of April's story as I stuffed them into my pocket. Hours later, in a sterile triage station, I remembered my friend Callie's essay, "In Defense of Mom Jeans"—where she wrote about a beloved pair of jeans she wore to her own D&C. She vividly described the act of slipping her clothes into a plastic bag, and I thought of her, and of that story, as I did the same.

Once home, still processing what had just happened to me, I recalled another essay Coffee + Crumbs published years ago, called "The Littlest Loss." A woman named Megan had written, "My baby was barely five weeks, the size of a sesame seed. Did I have a right to grieve such a small loss?"

Her words came to mind as I penned my own:

Seven weeks. It was enough time to dream, to wonder . . . boy or girl? Blue eyes or green? It was enough time to make plans to take a friend's hand-me-down car seat. Enough time to download one of those apps that tells you the baby is the size of a blueberry. It was enough time to fall in love.

After sharing publicly about my miscarriage on Instagram, I received a message from a woman named Jessica. She told me that one day, while praying for me, the Lord had brought an image to her mind. In the image, I was walking in a big grass field with a mowed path. I was all alone, tired and weary, and any time I needed to rest, a wood post would appear for me to lean against. She wrote, "I felt that post was the Lord saying He is there for you to lean on, exactly when you need Him."

Jessica said she couldn't figure out why I was all by myself, when in reality, she knew my husband and family and friends were supporting me through my loss.

"But then," she wrote, "I felt the Lord saying you were alone because nobody is experiencing this exactly like you. Your pain is unique, and He sees you. Then the Lord showed me if you look closely on the post there were engravings, the initials of other women who had come before you—other women who had used the Lord for support the same way you are right now."

Reading her message, I broke down sobbing. I could barely muster the words to convey how much her words meant to me, the powerful image she had just painted in my head. I shared the message with my husband and mastermind group, but no one else. In the grief-filled days to come, I would run to that picture for peace a hundred times.

Six weeks later, a flat cardboard envelope arrived on my doorstep, addressed to me. I opened it carefully, pulled out a print, and gasped. It was me. The field. The wooden post with initials.

In the midst of suffering a miscarriage, while writing a book about motherhood and creativity, God comforted me in real time— through art made by mothers.

After a few minutes of detective work, I learned my friend Sarah had commissioned the art from Aisha Branch, a fellow mom and artist. "That vision was too beautiful to forget," Sarah told me.

Aisha had taken such care in crafting the artwork, she even used initials from real women who had experienced miscarriages themselves, women who had left comments on my Instagram posts.

Not one of these details is lost on me. In the midst of suffering a miscarriage, while writing a book about motherhood and creativity, God comforted me in real time—through art made by mothers.

Running Coffee + Crumbs, I spent seven years reading about other women's miscarriages before I experienced my own. Many of those stories, in a way, comforted me in advance for my own future loss. The comfort I received propelled me forward to write about my own pain as it unfolded, compelling me to share a portion of my grief publicly, to add a cup of my own salty tears to the lake. Second Corinthians 1:4 tells us God comforts us in our afflictions, so that we can go forth and comfort others.

Through every vulnerability hangover, I prayed God would use my words. In the weeks that followed, I would receive dozens of messages from women all over the country, writing to me from doctors' offices and hospital beds, thanking me for putting language to this specific pain. For they, too, were in the process of miscarrying.

I will never get over the grace, the mercy, the wonder and mystery of it all, how God can use our creativity any second of any day, not only to inspire one another, but also to console our hearts before, during, and after they break.

I'VE ALWAYS THOUGHT OF CREATIVITY as an offering, like something you throw in the collection plate at church. If God's given me the gift of writing, anytime I share my words with the world, I'm giving a portion of my creative gifts back to God. In doing so, I surrender the work, releasing it back into the hands from which it came.

And here's where the creative process gets inexplicably good and mysterious. We will *never* know the full extent of what God does with our creative efforts. Whether our work inspires three people, twenty people, or a million; whether it impacts someone today, tomorrow, or eighteen years from now—what happens next is not up to us. When we open our hands and finally surrender a novel, or a mural, or a song, we acknowledge that the art is no longer ours. In a way, it never was.

Nothing we have belongs to us, but we can use everything we've been given to serve others, as messengers of God's grace.

Every day, God invites us to use our creativity to bless, inspire, and comfort others, the details of which we will never fully know or witness. In that sense, the art we create and share is just like the mustard seed. Our creative work starts out small, humble. And then, through the mystery of God, our creative efforts transform into something more significant and more meaningful than we could ever imagine, offering people hope, light, a refuge of shade on a hot summer day.

Our creative process is always and forever working in tandem with the Kingdom of God. Our role is to simply make the art, open our hands, and then wait and see what God does with it.

Who is God inviting you to share your creativity with? Maybe it's one person, a spouse or a family member. Maybe God's asking you to share your gifts with your local church or your neighborhood. Maybe He's asking you to be generous in your place of work or on social media.

AISHA BRANCH

ARTIST, ILLUSTRATOR, DESIGNER
@AISHABRANCH
LOS ANGELES, CALIFORNIA

Q: Do you have a Scripture, word, or mantra that guides your work?
A: There's a saying I heard in a movie once—"It's okay to cry . . . let the healing waters flow"—that helps me remember my *why*. My goal with the words I write, and the art I create, is to make someone feel safe and seen. People cry in both joyous moments and in pain, and one can experience healing and fullness through both. I want to use art as a way to exemplify God's heart toward those who need encouragement, or those who are too afraid to speak their struggles out loud. That quote, to me, speaks of vulnerability, but also healing, and that's how I want to show up with my art.

I don't know who He's calling you to serve, but I do know this: God does not give us gifts so we can hoard them. So write. Draw. Bake. Dance. Hand your baby to the one who is hurting.

Steward everything you've been given with care.

Be generous, open your hands in faith, and let God do the rest.

CREATIVE EXERCISE

Make something beautiful, and then give it away.

JOURNALING PROMPT

Who are the artists and creatives who have "fed the lake" or paved the way for you to create?

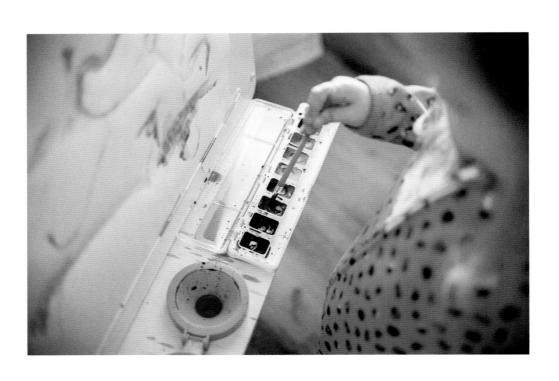

19

TRUST FALL

It's Friday morning and I'm sitting in my beloved rocking chair, sipping a mug of lukewarm coffee in Presley's room. We've already played with the plastic stacking cups, the music cube, and a handful of drool-covered teething toys. Now, with another hour until naptime, I'm simply watching Presley make her way around the room exploring on her hands and knees. At ten months old, she crawls over to the edge of her crib, grabs the railing, and slowly pulls herself up to standing, her latest trick.

With her left pudgy fist gripping one of the crib rails, she turns her head toward me, letting her right arm float out into space, as if she's standing on a tightrope. She bounces up and down for a few seconds, seeing how it feels, smiling, delighted with herself.

Her eyes lock with mine.

"You can do it," I half whisper, my eyes twinkling with encouragement. She looks at the floor. Back at me. Down at the floor. Back up at me. And then . . . *she lets go.*

Watching her, I'm reminded of the trust fall exercise we used to do as kids in PE class. We'd each get assigned a buddy, and then head out to the soccer field. (I always secretly hoped I'd get paired with my elementary school crush, a blue-eyed boy named Jason. I never did, prompting many dramatic entries in my Hello Kitty diary.) On the grass, each pair of students would face each other, and then one kid would turn around.

I don't remember the exact signal; was it a countdown? A whistle? Something would eventually alert us to fall backwards into the arms of our partner. The first time we'd fall, we'd be standing so close together, the fall felt more like a lean. But then we'd take one step forward and do it again. Then another step. And another.

The farther we stepped out, the scarier the fall, and the more we had to trust our partner. No matter how far we stepped out, though, we were always caught.

Presley stands on her own for a split second, triumphant with glee. In a flash, her knees buckle, and she hits the soft carpet with a gentle plop, looking startled for a moment before realizing she is fine. She smiles at me incredulously like, *Momma, can you believe I just did that?* And then she's off, crawling toward her next adventure.

ROUGHLY TWO YEARS AGO, I had an idea to create a narrative podcast exploring unconventional pathways to motherhood. I wanted to interview women who had overcome seemingly impossible circumstances to have a child, illustrating themes of hope, heartache, resilience, and redemption.

Minutes after I shared the concept publicly, I wondered if I was in over my head.

I'd never made a narrative podcast before. I was not familiar with the Five Act Structure—a common story framework used in projects like this. In addition to my overwhelming lack of experience, I had no

> Trust doesn't mean we will never fail,
> experience rejection, or embarrass
> ourselves trying something new.

clue who would host, edit, or produce the show. I didn't know how I'd fund such an expensive endeavor, or if anyone would even listen if I managed to get it off the ground.

I knew only one thing: *this* is how all creative ideas begin, with more questions than answers, more uncertainty than certainty, more doubt than confidence.

When I think back on every idea God's planted in my heart, every creative spark I've ever pursued, every little ladybug and breadcrumb I've followed, *trust* has been at the center of it all.

Trust doesn't mean every pursuit will become a smashing success. Trust doesn't mean we will never fail, experience rejection, or embarrass ourselves trying something new. But when we cross our arms in front of our chests, close our eyes, and lean back into the waiting arms of a God who loves us, we can rest in knowing both our hearts and dreams are in the very best hands.

Two years later, I still have more questions than answers about that narrative podcast. But I found an incredible host named Julie, who has both a heart of gold and relevant experience, and happens to live thirty minutes from my house (hello, breadcrumb!). Together we found ten courageous women willing to share their stories with us, and even though producing a show of this caliber has turned out to be a far greater undertaking than I realized, it's underway.

I've got other ideas in the works, too, tiny sparks just starting to catch fire. After greatly benefiting from my own mastermind group, I'm tinkering with the idea of developing some kind of workshop where I help small groups of women launch their own. A few friends and I chat regularly about someday opening a women's coworking space in our city. And of course, I'd love to keep growing in my photography skills. One day I'd love to be able to shoot an entire family session on film.

Right now, I don't know if any of these dreams or ideas will come to fruition. Saying them out loud—printing them in a book no less!—makes me nervous. *What if I never finish that podcast? What if I never pursue these dreams? What if I fail? What if? What if? What if?*

Andrew Peterson writes in *Adorning the Dark,* "Sometimes you start with nothing and hope it all works out. Not sometimes—*every* time. All you really have is your willingness to fail, coupled with the mountain of evidence that the Maker has never left nor forsaken you."[1]

In Exodus 3, God tells Moses he will play an essential role in leading the Israelites out of Egypt. Moses asks, "Who am I that I should go to Pharaoh and bring the children of Israel out of Egypt?"[2]

I can't tell you how many times I've asked God a similar question. *Who am I to lead this project? Who am I to pursue that endeavor? Who am I to write a book on motherhood and creativity? Is this a joke, Lord? Surely there is someone better!*

What I love about this scene in Exodus is that God does not respond by reassuring Moses that he is qualified for the task at hand. He doesn't say, "Moses, relax, you can totally do this!" Instead, God says, "But I will be with you"[3]—pointing Moses back to *Him.* To His sufficiency, His goodness, His plan.

Often when God calls me toward something new, the questions arrive quickly.

Do I have what it takes?

Am I willing to try?

(Am I willing to fail?)

Do I trust I'll be caught no matter what?

I take a few deep breaths. Then I close my eyes and lean back, remembering the mountain of evidence, the breadcrumbs, the ladybugs, and those six comforting words: "But I will be with you."

PRESLEY WILL BE THREE YEARS OLD in a few weeks. When I started writing this book, she could barely hold a crayon. Now she spends her days taking markers and colored pencils to any scrap of paper she can find. Printer paper. Unopened mail. Her brother's homework. She draws misshapen circles and blobs, often calling the finished piece her "family."

She then runs to me, waving the paper in her hand proudly. "Momma! I made dis for you!!!"

I consider all God made for us—light, language, sound, flowers that bloom, food that sizzles. A sun that rises and sets each day, stars that freckle the sky. Babies that coo and giggle and sigh contentedly against our chests. I continue to be astonished that God did not *need* to make any of this. He created the earth and all of mankind out of an abundance of love, an abundance of creativity.

And so it is with us.

Maybe you're at the beginning of a creative journey, just trying to work up the courage to start. Or maybe you're nearing the end, weary and exhausted, second guessing if you'll ever cross the finish line. Perhaps you're in the messy middle, wading through the muck, the fear, the insecurity.

Wherever you are, I pray you know—*your Maker is there too*, waiting with open arms.

At the time of writing this, we are still living in a global pandemic. I had a miscarriage nine weeks ago. A friend was just diagnosed with breast cancer. Another friend's entire life, as she knew it, is imploding before her eyes.

But, and. Just hours ago, another friend gave birth to a precious baby boy. And yet another is moving into her dream home this weekend. Such is life. Every day, sorrow and joy and pain and comfort swirl together like different colors of Play-Doh mixed into a ball—impossible to separate.

What can we even do, but search every battle cry for a melody?

I believe we have no choice but to hold this tie-dye mix of brokenness and grace in our palms, examining the beauty of its colors, looking for a rainbow, a promise. I believe we have no choice but to turn every hard and good thing over in our hands, adding a sprinkle of mercy, bending and shaping it into something new we can present to the world, some kind of art, some kind of masterpiece, as part of bearing witness to the glory of God alive in us.

I believe we have no choice but to keep going, to step out in faith as mothers and artists, with hope tucked under our arms, compassion and love on display.

I believe we have no choice but to create anyway.

ACKNOWLEDGMENTS

It takes a village to write a book, and I am forever indebted to mine.

To Jenni Burke, the best agent I could ever hope for, thank you for breathing confidence into my writing. Do you remember what you told me the night we looked at Christmas lights? I'll never forget that.

To Jennifer Dukes Lee, thank you for your careful guidance, enthusiasm, and commitment to putting ladybug icons on every piece of correspondence between us. Exclamation points will forever remind me of you (!!!). To the wonderful team at Bethany House, thank you for giving me a seat at the table, and for working tirelessly to make this book exactly what I wanted it to be. Deirdre, thank you for letting me be me.

To my beloved Coffee + Crumbs team, past and present, you make me a better storyteller, a better leader, and a better friend. *I wouldn't be here without you.* Thank you for spurring me on, for giving this book your blessing, and for holding down the fort while I wrote it. I love you, I love you, I love you.

To my "army" of beta readers: Ruth, Simone, Jodie, Adrienne, Cherise, Melissa, Kelsey, Meg—thank you for your valuable notes and ideas, but even more so, for your prayers and encouragement along the way.

To Jenna and Callie, thank you for pushing me, and for making these pages sing.

To Laura and Gretchen, thank you for the 742 pep talks.

To the friends who know me separate and apart from my work, the ones I eat and drink and travel with, the ones who have dropped off coffee and seen me without makeup and helped me become a mother—Lauren, Alli, Julie, Kristen, Anna, Kat, Kara, Dana, Katie, Lee, Christina—thank you for your friendship over the years.

To our Coffee + Crumbs Patrons, thank you for supporting me every time I've pursued mission over metrics. To our Exhale members, thank you for inspiring this entire book. I thought of you every time I sat down to write. To anyone who has been reading my work since the days of WMHR, you will never know how impossibly grateful I am for you. To the countless women who throw glitter on me on a regular basis, thank you for your endless encouragement. You are part of the reason I am still writing.

To Mom and Dad, thank you for always believing in me and for raising me to work hard at everything I do. (Dad, I suspect this book is going to be one more thing you brag about to strangers on airplanes. I am already embarrassed.) To Mitzie, thank you for throwing glitter on me and my work, time and time again. (I'd also like to thank you in advance for the seventy-five copies of this book I know you will buy.) To all three of you, especially Mom, thank you for the greatest gift of all—free babysitting.

(Which reminds me—special thanks to the PBS app, and specifically the makers of *Curious George* for entertaining Presley while I wrote this book. Also thank you to our babysitters, Avery and McLean.)

To my mastermind group, Sonya and Sarah and Katie, your fingerprints are on every page of this book. This accomplishment belongs to you as much as it belongs to me. Thank you for your edits, for listening to me cry, for not letting me give up. You call yourselves book doulas, but I call you my family. Katie, this book would not exist without you. Thank you for taking one look at my scribbled notes and texting back, "Ashlee, that's a book."

To Everett and Carson and Presley, my favorite masterpieces of all time, thank you for inspiring me with your wonder, your wild imaginations, and your own daily acts of creativity. I love being your mom.

And last but certainly not least: to Brett, my biggest champion, thank you for making the coffee every night so I could get up at 5:00 a.m. Thank you for the hundreds (thousands?) of sacrifices you've made over the past decade to support me in my work. Thank you for loving me so well, and for treating every one of my creative dreams as if it were your own. I love you.

NOTES

Introduction

1. Makoto Fujimura, *Art and Faith: A Theology of Making* (New Haven, CT: Yale University Press, 2020), 7.

2. Erwin Raphael McManus, *The Artisan Soul: Crafting Your Life into a Work of Art* (New York: HarperOne, 2014), 143.

3. Stephanie Duncan Smith, "Respect Your Reader," Slant Letter, April 7, 2021, https://stephanieduncansmith.substack.com/p/slant-letter-respect -your-reader.

Chapter 1 A Permission Slip

1. Genesis 2:15; 2:19

2. Anne Lamott, *Bird by Bird: Some Instructions on Writing and Life* (New York: Anchor Books, 1994), 191.

3. Jonathan Rogers, "A Note to Mothers," The Habit Weekly, https:// mailchi.mp/276bb78dd4b4/the-get-well-card-1658814?e=379c229b24.

4. Hunter Rawlings, "College Is Not a Commodity. Stop Treating It Like One," *The Washington Post*, June 9, 2015, www.washingtonpost.com/post everything/wp/2015/06/09/college-is-not-a-commodity-stop-treating-it-like -one.

Chapter 2 You Have Everything You Need

1. Luke 9:3

2. Ephesians 2:10 NIV

Chapter 3 Ready or Not

1. Madeleine L'Engle, *Walking on Water: Reflections on Faith and Art* (New York: Convergent Books, 2016), 54.

Chapter 4 Making Space

1. Makoto Fujimura, *Culture Care: Reconnecting with Beauty for Our Common Life* (Downers Grove, IL: InterVarsity Press, 2017), 15.

Chapter 5 Whose Voice Are You Listening To?

1. Genesis 3:9–11
2. Genesis 1:31
3. See Genesis 3:1
4. Neil Seligman, "Overcoming Imposter Syndrome," LinkedIn, October 18, 2021, www.linkedin.com/pulse/overcoming-imposter-syndrome-neil -seligman.

Chapter 6 Abundance over Scarcity

1. Matthew 25:14–30

Chapter 7 Breadcrumbs + Ladybugs

1. John 4:46–53
2. Lauren Winner, *Girl Meets God: On the Path to a Spiritual Life* (Chapel Hill, NC: Algonquin Books, 2002), 57.
3. Joanna Klein, "Ladybugs Pack Wings and Engineering Secrets in Tidy Origami Packages," *The New York Times*, May 18, 2017, www.nytimes.com /2017/05/18/science/ladybugs-wings-folding.html.

Chapter 8 Radical Obedience

1. Hannah Brencher, Write the Book course.
2. Julia Cameron, *The Artist's Way: A Spiritual Path to Higher Creativity* (New York, TarcherPerigee, 2016), 30.
3. Mark 14:6
4. Mark 14:8–9
5. Bob Sorge, *Secrets of the Secret Place: Keys to Igniting Your Personal Time with God* (Grandview, MO: Oasis House, 2001), 14.
6. NIV

Chapter 9 The Ark Didn't Build Itself

1. Shauna Niequist, *Bittersweet: Thoughts on Change, Grace, and Learning the Hard Way* (Grand Rapids, MI: Zondervan, 2010), 207–208.
2. Brian Doyle, *Leaping: Revelations & Epiphanies* (Chicago: Loyola Press, 2013), 12.
3. Erwin Raphael McManus, *The Artisan Soul: Crafting Your Life into a Work of Art* (New York: HarperOne, 2015), 130.

Chapter 10 Go Where the Light Is

1. Makoto Fujimura, *Culture Care: Reconnecting with Beauty for our Common Life* (Downers Grove, IL: InterVarsity Press, 2017), 51.
2. Brian Doyle, *Leaping: Revelations & Epiphanies* (Chicago: Loyola Press, 2013), 2.

Chapter 11 Nothing Is Wasted

1. Romans 8:28 NIV, emphasis mine

Chapter 12 It Takes a Village

1. Julia Cameron, *Finding Water: The Art of Perseverance* (New York: TarcherPerigee, 2009), 38.
2. Andrew Peterson, *Adorning the Dark: Thoughts on Community, Calling, and the Mystery of Making* (Nashville: B&H, 2019), 159.

Capter 13 Remember to Play

1. Julia Cameron, *The Artist's Way: A Spiritual Path to Higher Creativity* (New York: TarcherPerigee, 2016), 112.
2. Erwin Raphael McManus, *The Artisan Soul: Crafting Your Life into a Work of Art* (New York: HarperOne, 2015), 101.

Chapter 14 Fighting the Good Fight

1. Andrew Peterson, *Adorning the Dark: Thoughts on Community, Calling, and the Mystery of Making* (Nashville: B&H, 2019), 44.
2. Priscilla Shirer, *The Armor of God* (Nashville: Lifeway Press, 2015), 12.
3. Carey Wallace, "On Discipline," *Comment* magazine, September 1, 2001, https://comment.org/on-discipline.

Chapter 15 Throwing Glitter

1. David Burke, Fremont Presbyterian Church, Sacramento, California, October 31, 2021.
2. Julia Cameron, *The Right to Write: An Invitation and Initiation into the Writing Life* (New York: Tarcher/Putnam, 1998), 48.

Chapter 17 Rest

1. Jen Wilkin, *Ten Words to Live By: Delighting in and Doing What God Commands* (Wheaton, IL: Crossway, 2021), 65.

Chapter 18 Open Hands

1. Courtney Martin, "I Love. . . ," The Examined Family, October 20, 2021, https://courtney.substack.com/p/i-love.
2. Alex Dimitrov, "Love," *American Poetry Review*, https://aprweb.org/poems/love0.
3. Quoted in David Plante, *Difficult Women: A Memoir of Three* (New York: New York Review Books, 2017), 18.

Chapter 19 Trust Fall

1. Andrew Peterson, *Adorning the Dark: Thoughts on Community, Calling, and the Mystery of Making* (Nashville: B&H, 2019), 32.
2. Exodus 3:11
3. Exodus 3:12

ABOUT
THE AUTHOR

Ashlee Gadd is a wife, mother of three, and the founder of Coffee + Crumbs. When she's not working or vacuuming Cheerios out of the carpet, she loves making friends on the Internet, rearranging bookshelves, and eating cereal for dinner. You can find her online at ashleegadd.com and on Instagram @ashleegadd.

Coffee + Crumbs makes women feel safe, known, encouraged, and loved through artful, honest storytelling. To learn more, visit www.coffeeandcrumbs.net.